Hg2 Milan

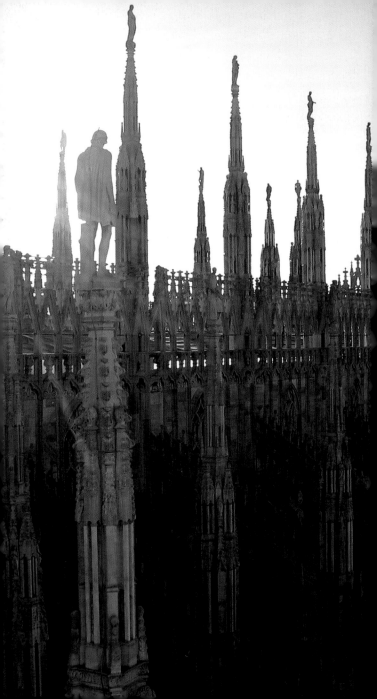

A Hedonist's guide to
Milan

BY Fleur Britten
PHOTOGRAPHY Fleur Britten

A Hedonist's guide to Milan

Managing director – Tremayne Carew Pole
Marketing director – Sara Townsend
Series editor – Catherine Blake
Design – P&M Design
Maps – Richard Hale
Typesetting – Dorchester Typesetting
Repro – PDQ Digital Media Solutions Ltd
Printer – Printed in Italy by Printer Trento srl
Publisher – Filmer Ltd

Email – info@ahedonistsguideto.com
Website – www.ahedonistsguideto.com

First published in the United Kingdom in June 2005 by
Filmer Ltd
47 Filmer Road
London SW6 7JJ

ISBN – 0-9547878-8-9

Hg2 Milan

CONTENTS

How to…

A Hedonist's guide to… is broken down into easy to use sections: Sleep, Eat, Drink, Snack, Party, Culture, Shop, Play and Info. In each of these sections you will find detailed reviews and photographs.

At the front of the book you will find an introduction to the city and an overview map, followed by descriptions of the four main areas and more detailed maps. On each of these maps you will see the places that we have reviewed, laid out by section, highlighted on the map with a symbol and a number. To find out about a particular place, simply turn to the relevant section, where all entries are listed alphabetically.

Alternatively, browse through a specific section (e.g. Eat) until you find a restaurant that you like the look of. Next to your choice will be a small coloured dot – each colour refers to a particular area of the city – then simply turn to the relevant map to discover the location.

Updates

Due to the lengthy publishing process and shelf lives of books it is very difficult to keep travel guides up to date – new restaurants, bars and hotels open up all the time, while others simply fade away or just go out of style. What we can offer you are free updates – simply log onto our website www.ahedonistsguideto.com or www.hg2.net and enter your details, answer a relevant question to provide proof of purchase and you will be entitled to free updates for a year from the date that you sign up. This will enable you to have all the relevant information at your finger tips whenever you go away.

In order to help us, if you have any comments or recommendations that you would like to see in the guide in future please feel free to email us at info@ahedonistsguideto.com.

The concept

A Hedonist's guide to… is designed to appeal to a more urbane and stylish traveller. The kind of traveller who is interested in gourmet food, elegant hotels and seriously chic bars – the traveller who feels the need to explore, shop and pamper themselves away from the madding crowd.

Our aim is to give you the inside knowledge of the city, to make you feel like a well-heeled, sophisticated local and to take you to the most fashionable places in town to rub shoulders with the local glitterati.

In today's world work rules our life, weekends away are few and far between, and when we do go away we want to have the most fun and relaxation possible with the minimum of stress. This guide is all about maximizing time. Everywhere is photographed, so before you go you know exactly what you are getting into; choose a restaurant or bar that suits you and your demands.

We pride ourselves on our independence and our integrity. We eat in all the restaurants, drink in all the bars and go wild in the nightclubs – all totally incognito. We charge no one for the privilege of appearing in the guide; every place is reviewed and included at our discretion.

We feel cities are best enjoyed by soaking up the atmosphere and the vibrancy; wander the streets, indulge in some retail relaxation therapy, re-energize yourself with a massage and then get ready to eat like a king and party hard on the stylish local scene.

We feel that it is important for you to explore a city on your own terms, while the places reviewed provide definitive coverage in our eyes; one's individuality can never be wholly accounted for. Sometimes if you take that little extra time to wander off our path, then you may just find that truly hidden gem that we missed.

Milan

The most over-used words in this guide are – unapologetically – chic and elegant. As Italy's fashion capital (spawning the likes of Giorgio Armani, Prada, Versace and Dolce & Gabbana), Milan is serried with sleek boutiques, smart bars, swanky restaurants and glamorous clubs. Its inhabitants' discerning tastes have pushed the envelope on design, vetoing foreign chains in favour of independent businesses. Milan is also a gateway to New York, Paris and London, and sets the pace for the rest of Italy. Residents compare it to New York's Upper East Side, with which it shares a similar sense of sophistication, decadence, snobbery and vanity, and a love of lounge bars, partying and Sunday brunches.

All year round, Milan is one big catwalk show and its residents pay punctilious attention to this season's fashion. A Milanese souvenir is most likely to be a pair of Prada shoes. However, the city remains notoriously provincial and conservative as it clings to its traditions and conventions; its fashion designers have thankfully filled a void by branching out with hip new bars, spas, restaurants and clubs.

Predictably, budget is not a familiar word in Italy's richest city (and second largest, with a population of 1.2 million). As Italy's financial capital and home to Italy's stock exchange, its media capital, home to the country's main advertising agencies, four national daily newspapers, major publishing houses and Berlusconi's media empire; and design capital: with its annual furniture fair, La Fiera, plus a heritage of eminent architects, Milan has staked out its position as a world-class design centre.

While Milan is dismissed as a cultural destination (buffs would head first to Rome, Florence or Venice), its relatively low count of highlights makes them perfectly manageable in a weekend; its compact size makes it easily negotiable by foot. Aesthetically it's an eclectic city –

some say ugly, because of a heavy industrial influence and arguably ill-judged rapid post-war expansion. Its architecture is a veritable timeline from the Roman Empire to the present, via Romanesque, Renaissance, neoclassical, *belle epoche* and Fascist eras. And Milan certainly has charm, thanks to its canals, cobbled streets and antique tram system,

but it also has a dire pollution problem because of its position in the wind-free Po Valley and its proliferation of industrial plants.

An ancestry of wealth predicates Milan's rather snobbish manner, where social strata are regarded as importantly as fashion labels. Thus, '*Milanese*' is a byword for the middle-class (since that's the majority in Milan); then there's the *borghesi* (bourgeois) and the *fighetti*, the idle rich offspring of old Milanese money. The *Hinterland* are those in surrounding suburbia and the *terroni* (from the soil) hail from Southern Italy; both are treated as second-class citizens (as indeed are tourists and Milan's immigrant community from China, Senegal, Sri Lanka, etc.). Of course, willowy international models and imported architects and fashion designers are considered great assets to the city.

Geographically, Milan lends itself well to a lifestyle of country retreats, weekend skiing, and summertime water sports. During the summer, high humidity and temperatures effect a centrifugal force on its residents and the whole city heads out to its border attractions to relax with *aperitivo* – another word that repeatedly crops up throughout this book. *Aperitivo* – or Milan's daily ritual of after-work drinks and free food – suggests in a word the kind of quality of life that is enjoyed in Milan.

0   1km   2km

SLEEP

9. Enterprise Hotel

EAT

12. Chatulle
20. Don Juan
21. Eda
22. Fingers
27. Il Luogo di Aimo E Nadia
31. Quattrocento
35. Shambala

DRINK

2. Alchimia
5. B4
26. Roïalto

SNACK

11. Gattullo

CULTURE

12. Auditorium di Milano

PARTY

7. Il Gattopardo Café
9. Karma / Borgo del Tempo Perso
11. Magazzini Generali
16. Rocket

Centro

Milan's small, compact nucleus is split neatly into two: the north-east half, comprising the fashion heart, or *quadrilatero d'oro*, and the south-west – the cultural heart, or *centro storico*. The *quadrilatero d'oro* (golden rectangle) is so-called for its dense concentration of designer fashion stores – the world's highest, apparently. Bound within the equivalent of four Bond Streets are hundreds of boutiques from the world's most powerful fashion houses. Of course beyond the *quadrilatero d'oro* virtually every other brand is accounted for as they vie for profits from the vast volumes of tourist traffic. All the way from Via Dante (which connects the centre to the castle), along the long porticoes of Piazza del Duomo and through to Corso Vittorio Emanuele II, are yet more boutiques from high street to high fashion. It's easy to see how Milan is Italy's commercial capital with the volume of consumerism indulged in here.

The *centro storico* (historical centre) is mostly pedestrianized – apparently the largest car-free city centre in Europe and home to some of Milan's awesome sights. Right at the centre is the world's third largest cathedral, the Gothic white marble Duomo, which took four centuries to build, and the Galleria Vittorio Emanuele II, a 19th-century shopping

arcade *par excellence*, with its much-imitated glass and steel arched and domed roof. Milan's peerless opera house Teatro alla Scala is also in the zone, as are numerous important museums and galleries, including the museum-cum-homes Museo Poldi Pezzoli and Museo Bagatti Valsecchi, the 18th-century neo-classical Palazzo Reale, which contains treasures from the Austrian empire, 19th-century novelist Alessandro Manzoni's open house, and the museums of La Scala and the Duomo.

Totemic statues stand majestically in the Centro's grand open squares – in Piazza del Duomo  is a horse-mounted monument to Vittorio Emanuele II, Italy's first king after unification in 1861. In Piazza della Scala is a vast bronze of honorary Milanese resident Leonardo da Vinci. All over the centre, modern sculptures are set against historic backdrops: here the old and the new sit side-by-side more so than anywhere else in the rest of Milan. The centre also comprises Milan's commercial district, just south of the *quadrilatero d'oro* are gleaming glass office blocks and corporate headquarters.

As Italy's financial capital, Milan's financial heart also beats right here, with La Borsa Stock Exchange in Piazza Affari. The first stock exchange was established at Monte di Pietà in 1808 to meet the financial demands of the textile industry and was so successful that it has out-grown itself three times – this neoclassical 1930s building is now in its fourth incarnation.

The large influx of rich tourists heavily laden with this season's fash-ions are amply catered for by some of Milan's best five-star hotels, such as the Four Seasons, the Park Hyatt Milano, the Grand Hotel et de Milan and the Gray. Just about everything here, from tea salons like Cova and Peck, indulgent restaurants such as Nobu and Il Teatro, old-money clubs such as Nepentha, and chichi fashion bars, including Marino alla Scala and Dolce & Gabbana's Martini Bar, is Milan at its most showy.

```
0        250m        500m
|————————|————————|
```

M Metro Station

EAT

6.	Armani/Nobu
7.	Bagutta
9.	Boeucc
16.	Cracco-Peck
17.	Da Bice
30.	Parco
34.	A Santa Lucia
37.	Il Teatro

SLEEP

2.	Alle Meraviglie
5.	Antica Locanda Mercanti
8.	Carlton Hotel Baglioni
11.	Four Seasons Hotel
12.	Grand Hotel et de Milan
13.	Grand Hotel Duomo
14.	The Gray
15.	Hotel de la Ville
16.	Hotel Dei Cavalieri
20.	Hotel Spadari
21.	Hotel Straf
22.	Park Hyatt Milano

SHOP

	Corso Venezia
	Via della Spiga
	Via Manzoni
	Via Montenapoleone
	Via Sant' Andrea
2.	Armani
3.	Peck

CULTURE

4.	Duomo
5.	Galleria d'Arte Moderna and PAC
6.	Galleria Vittorio Emanuele II
8.	Museo Poldi Pezzoli
11.	Teatro Alla Scala

Garibaldi and Parco Sempione

Parco Sempione and Garibaldi are two neighbouring districts, quite distinct in history and atmosphere. Parco Sempione encompasses wealthy West Milan with Castle Sforza as its nucleus. Garibaldi is in fact three incrementally industrial yet increasingly fashionable districts stacked northwards on top of each other and connected by Corso Garibaldi – Brera, Corso Como and Isola.

Within the park itself (Milan's largest and most important, designed by Alemagna in the 19th century) are La Triennale, the 1930s fascist-style design museum, and Torre Branca, Milan's mini-answer to the Eiffel Tower; latched onto the east side is the Arena, the Napoleonic amphitheatre. Hip new bars are cropping up around the park as well as the newly gentrified Chinatown (Italy's largest). A prime spot is by the Arco della Pace, which was designed by Cagnola and erected between 1801 and 1814 for Napoleon and dedicated to peace in 1815 after Napoleon's fall. Further out west is the San Siro football stadium and La Fiera, the vast exhibition halls that host Milan's world-famous furniture fair each year (although plans to move it elsewhere are underway). And along Via Magenta to the southwest is Leonardo da Vinci's ghostly *Last Supper* fresco in a Renaissance church refectory, and numerous aristocratic houses such as Palazzo degli Atellani where musicians and artists including Da Vinci were received as guests, and Palazzo Arese Litta, the 17th-century family residence of the Areses and then the Littas. More noble mansions stand along the tree-lined boulevards between Corso Magenta and Parco Sempione. To the east of Parco Sempione is the Cimitero Monumentale, the graveyard preserved for Milan's richest inhabitants.

In between Parco Sempione and the *centro storico* is Brera, a charming historic quarter containing the Pinocateca di Brera (Milan's most important art gallery) and all the artsy crowds that flock to it. A well-preserved labyrinth of windy cobbled streets with hidden palazzos and art galleries, bars, restaurants and cafés entice a large tourist crowd. The Milanese prefer to hang out in Corso Como, a short pedestrianised street that starts at the grand neo-classical arch of Porta Garibaldi and finishes at Garibaldi Station. This is Club Central, with eight clubs and plenty of warm-up bars and pizzerias. Since fashion muse Carla Sozzani opened her lifestyle concept store here, other fashion boutiques have followed suit, and by day it's also a select, high-end retail zone.

North of the station is Isola. Its name, 'island', originates from its enclave status since it is hemmed in by Garibaldi's railway; its residents think of it as a small town inside a larger town and share an endearing community spirit. Life here is far removed from the ways of the centre – while it previously has not been refined or safe, it's always been bohemian. Isola is unique in Milan for having more relaxed planning regulations and gentrification is fast changing its industrial landscape. The last five years have seen Isola becoming more friendly and trendy, a move that is set to continue with the arrival of the Città della Moda in 2010 – a fashion city complete with catwalk, museum, school, library etc. Isola's nightlife (centered around Via Borsieri and including two semi-legal egalitarian squats) is attracting the liberal types that previously characterized Navigli.

Via Cenisio
Via L. Nono
Via Messina
Via Losanna
Via Castelvetro
Via Monviso
Via Tartaglia
Via Procaccini
Via Piero della Francesca
Corso Sempione
Via Fioravanti
Via Paolo Lomazzo
Via Paolo Sarp
Via Mussi
V. Bertini
Via L. Canonica
V.F.Londonio
Corso Sempione
V. Moscati
Via Giusti
Via Melzi d'Eril
Via Massena
Via Pucci
Via Bertani
Via Abbondio Sangiorgio
Viale Malta
Via Machiavelli
Via Reg. Savoia Cav.
Via V. Monti
Viale Zola
V. Emilio Alemagna
Via Gadi
Via Mario Pagano
Via Ari
Via
Via Petrarca
Via Zola
Via Telesio
Via Aristoto
Via Tasso
V. XX Settembre
Via Leopardi
Via V. Monti
Via Rasori
Via Boccaccio
Via Ruffini
Via Saffi
Corso Vercelli
Corso Magenta

0   250m   500m

M Metro Station

SNACK

3.	Biffi
5.	Cantiere dei Sensi
6.	Chocolat
7.	Coffee Design
10.	Fioraio Bianchi Caffè
13.	Mediateca Caffetteria Degli Atellani
15.	Princi
16.	San Carlo

CULTURE

2.	Castello Sforzesco
3.	Cimitero Monumentale
7.	The Last Supper
9.	Pinocateca di Brera
10.	La Triennale di Milano

PARTY

2.	The Black
6.	Gasoline
8.	Hollywood
10.	Loolapaloosa
13.	Old Fashion Café
14.	Pergola Move
17.	Shocking
18.	Soul to Soul
19.	Tocqueville 13
20.	Blue Note

SLEEP

1.	3Rooms
4.	Antica Locanda Leonardo
6.	Antica Locanda Solferino
7.	The Bulgari Hotel
26.	UNA Hotel Tocq

Porta Romana and Porta Venezia

On the east side of the city are the triumphal arches of Porta Venezia (north-east) and Porta Romana (south-east) — two of Milan's city gates originally built as 16th-century Spanish fortifications and repeatedly rebuilt through history. Needless to say, you can head for Venice (east) by one, or for Rome (south-east) by the other.

The area around Porta Venezia is at once commercial, residential, historic and ethnic. To the south-east of the fascist monument Stazione Centrale are Middle Eastern, North African, Senegalese and Indian ghettoes, characterized by textile cottage industries and ethnic food outlets. On course for Monza is Corso Buenos Aires with over 3km of high-street chains and factory outlets.

Also a major traffic artery of Milan, Corso Venezia houses the other end of the retail spectrum with high fashion boutiques carried over from the *quadrilatero d'oro.* Look up, and there is an entirely different scene: historic aristocratic townhouses, from 15th-century Renaissance residences and 18th-century neoclassical houses to 19th-century neo-Palladian palazzos and turn-of-the-century Liberty façades (including the remarkable Palazzo Castiglioni); right at Porta Venezia is the Hotel Diana, famous for its Liberty features.

On the west side of Corso Venezia is Milan's second biggest central park, Giardini Pubblici. Built in the 18th century by neo-classical architect Giuseppe Piermarini (who also designed La Scala and the Palazzo Reale), it was extended by Parco Sempione's architect Alemagna in the next century to include the neo-classical Villa Reale, an ex-royal abode topped with toga-ed statues that now houses the Galleria d'Arte Moderna. The park also contains Milan's natural history museum

Civico Museo di Storia Naturale, the Museo del Cinema and the Planetario Ulric Hoepli. At the south end of Corso Venezia is the Basilica di San Babila, a Romanesque church first built in the 4th century, just at the edge of the commercial centre of Milan.

Porta Romana is situated in the middle of the thoroughfare Corso di Porta Romana, which heads south-east from Piazza Missori in the *centro* past the University of Milan and through the Piazzale Medaglie d'Oro, where the remains of the old 16th-century Spanish walls and the arch itself lie. While the area is both residential and industrial, Porta Romana is also punctuated by lots of fashionable bars, clubs and restaurants. Their distance away from the more commercial zones of the Centro, Corso Como and Navigli serves as a positive index of how hip a venue is, culminating in a cluster of fashionable establishments at the south end of Via Ripamonti (which splits off from Porta Romana). In between Porta Venezia and Porta Romana and heading due east is Corso di Porta Vittoria – of which several blocks are taken out by the majestic fascist architecture of Palazzo di Giustizia, Milan's law courts, where some of Italy's most important court cases are heard. Further east on this road is the historic monument to five very important days in Milan's history in March 1848 (at Piazza 5 Giornate), when the whole of Milan demonstrated against Austrian rule, capturing the official government buildings and driving out the Hapsburg officials. Now a mighty sculpture and obelisk stand proud in the square in honour of the fallen.

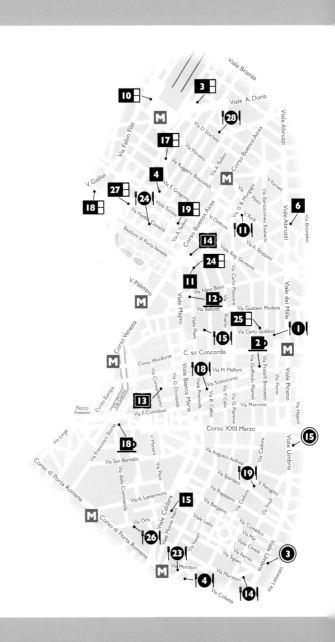

0   0.5   1km

M Metro Station

EAT

1. 13 Giugno
4. Altro Spazio Strato
11. Chandelier
14. Compagnia Generale
15. Controvapore
18. Da Giacomo
19. Dar el Yacout
23. Giulio Pane e Ojo
24. Joia
26. Lifegate Restaurant
28. Milch

PARTY

3. Café Atlantique
15. Plastic

SLEEP

3. Anderson
10. Excelsior Hotel Gallia
17. Hotel Mediolanum
18. Hotel Principe di Savoia
19. Hotel Sanpi
24. Sheraton Diana Majestic
25. Townhouse 31
27. The Westin Palace

SHOP

Via Durini

CULTURE

13. Conservatorio di
    Musica 'Giuseppe Verdi'

DRINK

4. Atomic
6. Bar Basso
11. Diana Garden
15. Fresco Art

SNACK

2. L'Arte di Offrire il Thé
12. Grand Café a Tre Marie
18. Taveggia

Navigli

The Navigli area comprises what is left of Milan's canal system (*'navigli'* means 'canals') – now just two long canals and a dock, located south of the city centre. Milan's entrepreneurs have capitalized on its canalside prettiness, making Navigli the stomping-ground of the city's youth.

Fifteen years ago, the neighbourhood was characterized by bohemia: artists, musicians, poets, etc.; now it's much less underground, but Navigli remains atmospheric, with a thriving nightlife and street scene. If subcultures (punks, Goths, graffiti kids, and the like) are to be seen anywhere in Milan, the chances are highest here. Navigli is spared the gloss of the Centro, making for an authentic window into old Milan. Old washhouses and tenement buildings line the canals, many of which are now art ateliers and antique shops, and old barges are moored up as cafés and overspills to the canalside bars and clubs.

Boat trips can be taken up the 50km long Naviglio Grande (the more western canal) to the village of Gaggiano, past classical houses and old mechanical features designed by Leonardo da Vinci (see Play). Work on the Naviglio Grande began in 1177 and was completed in 1257; it took as its source the Ticino river, which lies south-west of Milan, and finished in the Darsena (docks) alongside Viale Gorizia. The other,

Naviglio Pavese, was built in stages from the 14th century till 1819, and flows out for 33km from the Darsena back into the Ticino. Originally, Milan's waterways were a citywide medieval structure built to ferry the marble building blocks from the quarries of Candoglia to the Duomo. The canal system also provided irrigation for the plains of Lombardy and served as an important trade link between the north and south, connecting a landlocked city to the country's ports. In 1929, Milan's canal network was mostly filled in to make way for roads as barges were superseded by road travel.

Now, Navigli is an eclectic patchwork of old and new. At its heart is Porta Ticinese, where the two canals and the docks meet; here traders were originally marshalled by two imposing pale yellow *dazi* (customs houses) that still preside at the centre of the action (although one contains a raucous bar and the other a Communist club). The main strip, Corso di Porta Ticinese, is packed with young, jeansy shops and hip yet cheap restaurants and bars, and leads north to the ancient Roman Colonne di San Lorenzo – 16 Corinthian columns that flank the church of San Lorenzo Maggiore. To the west is Porta Genova, an up-and-coming area where lots of fashion designers and photographers have opened studios. Also west is one of Milan's most important churches, the Basilica of Sant' Ambrogio, built in AD 386 by Milan's patron saint, Ambrose. The two *navigli* themselves are crowded with tourists and students, who populate the bars, restaurants, cafés, art galleries, record shops, artisan boutiques and junk shops. Once a month is the Mercatone dell'Antiquariato along the Naviglio Grande, an antiques market selling bric-à-brac and collectibles. In the summer, the Navigli is besieged by cool crowds as both close to traffic after 8.30pm and canalside bars and cafés stay open till late for jazz and other live music.

Via C. da Sesto
Via Aus
Viale Papiniano
Viale Coni Zugna
Via Bergognone
Via Tortona
Via Vigeva.
Via Tortona
Strada Alzaia Naviglio Grande
Ripa di Porta Ticinese
Via Autari
Via Filippo Argelati
Via Pastorelli
Via Carlo Torre
Via Giovanni
Viale Cassala
Viale Liguria
Via Valsolda

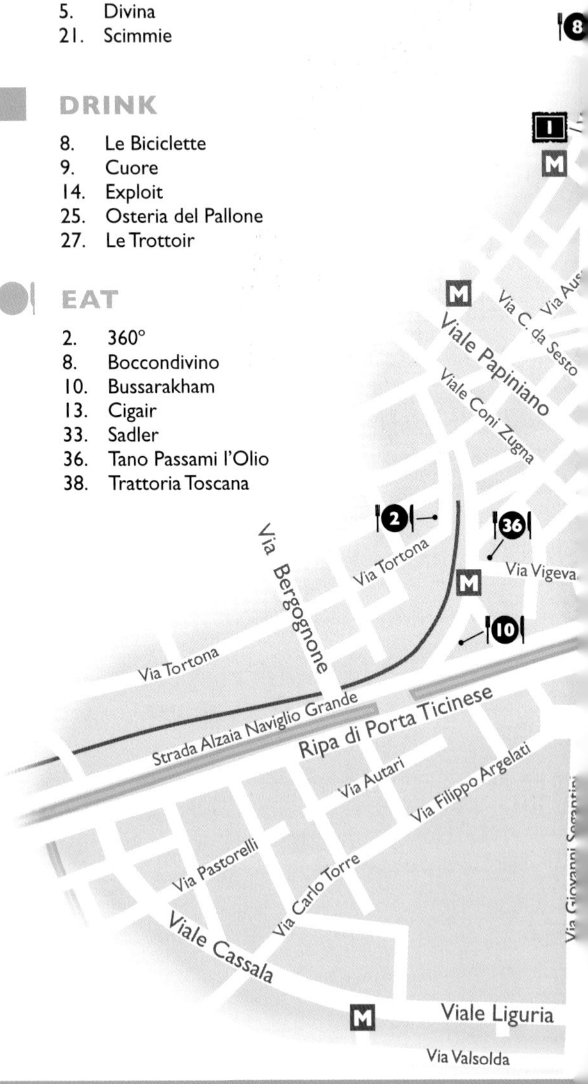

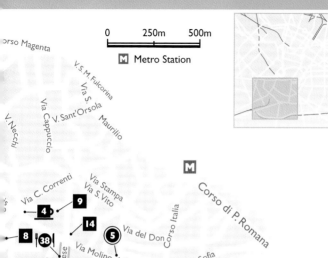

0   250m   500m

M Metro Station

Corso Magenta

V.S. M. Fulcorina

Via Cappuccio

Via S. Maurilio

V. Sant'Orsola

V. Nechi

Via C. Correnti

Via Stampa

Via S. Vito

4

9

14

Corso Italia

Corso di P. Romana

8

38

5

Via del Don

Via Arena

Corso di Porta Ticinese

Via Molino delle Armi

Via S. Sofia

13

23

Via Mercalli

Via S. Croce

Corso Italia

27

5

Naviglio Grande Ascanio Sforza

Corso S. Gottardo

21

33

Via G. Meda

SLEEP

23. Petit Palais

SHOP

Corso di Porta Ticinese

SNACK

4. Caffè della Pusterla

CULTURE

1. Basilica di Sant 'Ambrogio

sleep...

In a city powered by fashion and design, it's surprising to discover a relative absence of design hotels. It's even more peculiar considering Milan's abundance of accomplished architects and reputation for discerning style. But most hotels cater for businessmen who come to Milan to make money all year round. The corporate hotels are generally focused around the Stazione Centrale and to a lesser extent in Piazza Repubblica (where Milan's main station used to be).

Fortunately Milan has been under the developer's spotlight in the new millennium thanks to increasing awareness of this design hotel demand-supply skew. New hotels have sprung up all over Milan like it's winning a game of Monopoly, with 'haute hotels' such as the Bulgari Hotel (the jeweller's first foray into hospitality) and the Park Hyatt Milano both taking their lead from erstwhile *numero uno* super-luxe hotel The Four Seasons. Other newcomers are high fashion hotels the Gray and Hotel Straf, and boutique hotels such as 3Rooms, Townhouse 31 and 12, and Petit Palais.

Another trend is the *antica locanda* (or old-fashioned inn); in chic Milan that means a boutique-style bed-and-breakfast. *Antiche locande* Leonardo, Solferino and Mercanti, and the Mercanti's neighbour, Alle Meraviglie – situated in historic townhouses – are charmingly and sympathetically styled and all give the feeling

of being a guest in someone's house; staff retire when guests do, so receptions are only manned during the day; some offer night porters, others provide keys. Mod-cons are not givens in these more modest establishments, often because their landlords are resolute Luddites.

Some of the most important hotels in Milan are the oldest; here, guests can most assimilate real Milanese culture. Grand Hotel et de Milan and Hotel Principe di Savoia both compete for the crown of grandeur. Some have forsaken modern improvements for conservation reasons (the Liberty-style Sheraton Diana Majestic is one such behemoth). Other bastions have modernized along the way, often resulting in clashing styles.

Visitors can assume a four-star-plus hotel room will come equipped with a safe, fridge/minibar, aircon, noise insulation, satellite- and pay-TV, direct phone, laundry services, internet access and conference facilities. Milan's high season is during its world-famous furniture fair La Fiera in April. Bookings need to made well in advance and hotels can charge cancellation fees up to a month in advance over this period. Nevertheless, don't be deterred by the human traffic – this is Milan at its most fun. In August, Milan's low season, room prices plummet – but be warned that during this month the city becomes a ghost town as the Milanese vacate to the beach; most restaurants, bars and clubs close. The only people left are tourists that got a suspiciously good deal through their travel agent.

The rates quoted here are for a standard double in low season and a one-bedroom suite in high season. All hotels are scored for style, atmosphere and location (highest scorers are near the Duomo, Milan's nucleus). If it seems that most don't seem to offer much atmosphere, it's probably because of the relative weighting of corporate clients; generally Milan's hotels have also been slow – unlike Paris, London and New York – to catch onto the hip hotel bar, and most of these are not made for hanging out in.

Our top ten hotels in Milan are:
1. The Bulgari Hotel
2. The Four Seasons
3. Park Hyatt Milano
4. Grand Hotel et de Milan
5. The Gray
6. Hotel Straf
7. Townhouse 31
8. Alle Meraviglie
9. Hotel Principe di Savoia
10. Anderson

Our top five hotels for style are:
1. The Gray
2. The Bulgari Hotel
3. 3Rooms
4. Hotel Straf
5. Anderson

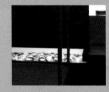

Our top five hotels for atmosphere are:
1. Townhouse 31
2. Antica Locanda Leonardo
3. Petit Palais
4. Antica Locanda Solferino
5. Hotel Spadari

Our top five hotels for location are:
1. Park Hyatt Milano
2. The Four Seasons
3. Carlton Hotel Baglioni
4. Grand Hotel Duomo
5. The Bulgari Hotel

3Rooms, Corso Como, 10, Garibaldi
Tel: 02 626 263 www.3rooms-10Corsocomo.com
Rates: €295

Carla Sozzani's hotel offshoot of her cult fashion emporium (see Shop and Drink) is the ultimate statement in exclusivity: a 3rooms door key automatically grants access to the cool club, and of course there are only three keys to be had. Actually it's more like 3apartments, each with a living room, set on the first floor of Sozzani's palazzo complex, overlooking a cobbled, leafy courtyard. All are decorated in Corso Como's signature mono-chromatic ethno-urban style and packed with iconic 20th-century design pieces. Everything in these showroom suites is available to buy: Eames chairs, Castiglioni lights, B&O TVs, DVD players and music systems, Porsche kettles, etc. In fact buying is so encouraged, it's as if staying here were merely an after-hours shopping opportunity. All suites come with weights for closet exercising (which is telling of 3Rooms' client profile). Officially a bed-and-breakfast, there's no common area or night-time recep-tion. But guests of 3rooms can of course indulge in the facilities of the on-site café and restaurant, and in true *Ab Fab* style be first in line for tomorrow's fashion.

Style 9, Atmosphere 8, Location 8

Alle Meraviglie, Via San Tomaso, 8, Centro
Tel: 02 805 1023   www.allemeraviglie.it
Rates: €145–305

Loosely translated as full of wonder, Alle Meraviglie is indeed an enchanting set-up in just six beautifully appointed rooms on the second and third floor of a genteel townhouse. Fittingly, the architect's brief was to surprise, so, while sympathetic to the building's history with tasteful 19th-century antiques, there's a bit

of drama, such as shocking pink raw silk curtains (though now no longer a surprise). Under the same management as Antica Locanda Mercanti (which is next door; see page 34), it shares many similarities: it's big on light, space, individuality, fresh flowers and literature, and very small on ugly urbanities such as TVs (although wifi is – invisibly – available in all rooms). It's equally fragrant and equally hidden with no street sign; the reception – like a whitewashed Victorian parlour with flowers in enamel milk pails – is manned from 7am until 11pm, and staff are happy to attend to most requests. And with an extra star rating (four star), it's extra special.

Style 9, Atmosphere 8, Location 8

Anderson, Piazza Luigi di Savoia, 20, Porta Venezia
Tel: 02 669 0141   www.starhotels.it
Rates: €199–369

The luxurious four-star Anderson, renovated in 2004 by the Starhotels chain, is styled to within an inch of its life like a Wallpaper* bachelor pad. The look is super-sleek, with black lacquered furniture, blood red carpets, zebra skins, exotic flowers and a B&O entertainment system, and in the 'library', a statement fireplace and untouched recherché books. The

restaurant/bar, 'Black', is predictably deep black and deeply chic. Its 106 rooms are equally modern and variously decorated in cream marble, chrome, wenge wood, leather panelling and black-and-white photography; mod-cons stretch to 6-inch TV monitors in every bathroom. Its proximity to the Stazione Centrale, ample conference facilities and fitness room attract a (well-groomed) business clientele, accessorized with all the latest executive toys. The Anderson, somewhere in between cool and cold, gives the inside track to a Milanese idiosyncrasy: temptingly fashionable yet haughty and affected.

Style 9, Atmosphere 7, Location 7

Antica Locanda Leonardo, Corso Magenta, 78, Parco Sempione
Tel: 02 463 317 www.leoloc.com
Rates: €135–240

In a 19th-century flower-filled nobleman's house, set back from

the street through a private courtyard, is the Leonardo, run by husband-and-wife team Mario and Chiara (her real Japanese name is Yumi but there is no 'y' in Italian). This friendly bed-and-breakfast is so-called because Chiara spent three long years translating a book on Da Vinci, and it attracts many art fans because of its proximity to his *Last Supper*. It comprises 20 three-star rooms on three floors (no lift, to preserve the *antica* feel). All are different in style: some are modern Japanese, some traditional Italian with repro antiques, some even with Chiara's own art; all with cherrywood parquet floors and modest bathrooms. The best have a balcony overlooking the garden, which is full of flowers and foliage and white wrought-iron garden furniture. The common areas are homely: a living room with comfy velvet sofas, and a dainty breakfast salon and bar, where tea and cakes, *aperitivo* and Mario's potent grappa coffees are served.

Style 7, Atmosphere 8, Location 8

Antica Locanda Mercanti, Via San Tomaso, 6, Centro
Tel: 02 805 4080 www.locanda.it
Rates: €155–255

So-called because merchants used to frequent this inn a century ago, there is nothing businessy about the three-star Antica Locanda Mercanti now. In fact, it's exemplary of Milan's *locande*: immaculate, homely and full of character. Scented with fresh flowers, it has the feel of a summer villa – right in the heart of the *centro storico* in an unmarked townhouse hidden in a street of antique shops. There are 13 unique architect-designed rooms, all with crisp white bedlinen, plenty of light, and fresh flowers in the place of a TV (TVs are available on request, but it's more fitting to bury one's nose in one of the one-night-read communal books). It's worth upgrading to a terrace room with private garden, variously filled with aromatic herbs, geraniums and potted trees. All four terrace rooms come with aircon; standard rooms have ceiling fans. After all, it's essentially a simple and friendly guesthouse (reception is staffed from 7am until 11pm) that refuses to call itself a hotel.

Style 8, Atmosphere 8, Location 8

Antica Locanda Solferino, Via Castelfidardo, 2, Garibaldi
Tel: 02 657 0129   www.anticalocandasolferino.it
Rates: €100–220

The romantic Antica Locanda Solferino used to be an inn for couples wanting to 'get a room'. Now, endearingly decorated with early 20th-century antiques, crisp sheets and floral quilts, it's more like staying in granny's guest bedroom. All 11 rooms in this Napoleonic building in Brera are different, variously adorned with *broderie anglaise* curtains, lace doilies, antique dressers and original shutters and radiators. Amenities are simple, with TVs in

all rooms and aircon in some. There are no public areas, just a flower-filled reception in the hallway (serviced from 7am until 11pm), attached to a trattoria that supplies the room service; the friendly staff will oblige most other requests. Breakfast in bed is obligatory since there's no breakfast room – cute for weekend-ing couples. For complete privacy, the *locanda* has two stylish apartments in Via San Marco, rather removed from its olde-worlde charm with late 1960s designer furniture.

Style 8, Atmosphere 8, Location 8

The Bulgari Hotel, Via Privata Fratelli Gabba, 7/B, Garibaldi
Tel: 02 805 8051 www.bulgarihotels.com
Rates: €450–3,500

Bulgari – international byword for luxury – opened its first hotel in Milan in summer 2004. With its first-class bar, a large land-scaped garden and one of the city's best spas, uptown Milan has mobbed the place. Superbly located in a secluded private street in Brera near to the *quadrilatero d'oro*, the five-star Bulgari hotel stands proud in a 1950s Bauhaus-inspired white marble building. Inside has considerable wow factor: bold and contemporary, in strong organic colours of chocolate and charcoal. The 58 rooms and six suites are softer, all with oak, bronze and matt black mar-ble, B&B Italia furniture, Frette linen (Italy's finest), 28-inch flat-screen TVs, and of course Bulgari toiletries. The staff is ready for action in brown safari suits and hoodies: service is impeccable, with complimentary packing/unpacking, playstations on request, and even Ferrari car hire (or see Play), should you need to bolster your power rating among a clientele of barons, moguls and tycoons. Because at this price, the Bulgari says – in a discreet whisper – money.

Style 9, Atmosphere 8, Location 9

Carlton Hotel Baglioni, Via Senato, 5, Centro
Tel: 02 770 77 www.baglionihotels.com
Rates: €275–935

A member of the Leading Small Hotels of the World, this five-star hotel calls itself the city's 'drawing room' (a moniker in fact borrowed from Milan's 19th-century Galleria shopping arcade). The Baglioni is stately but not grand – thanks to low ceilings and the welcoming aroma of log fires – and is decorated in turn-of-last-century antique statuettes, Persian rugs, crystal chandeliers and silk brocades. Its gentlemanly library is the perfect place to affect old-fashioned traditions with a pipe in front of the fireplace. Art-deco touches, such as rosewood marquetry on doors and marble mosaic floors, attract the style *savants*, also wise to the doorstep shopping opportunities here (its back entrance leads to Via della Spiga). Guests pay a premium on the 92 small, soundproofed rooms, though suites have large private terraces. With a piano bar and the famous Il Baretto restaurant that joined the hotel in 2003 after 42 years on Via Sant' Andrea, the Baglioni is a trusty old stalwart in the heart of a fickle fashion world.

Style 8, Atmosphere 7, Location 9

Enterprise Hotel, Corso Sempione, 91, Parco Sempione
Tel: 02 318 188 34   www.enterprisehotel.com
Rates: €121–690

Hailed when it first opened in spring 2002 as an innovative design hotel, the Enterprise, built in an old 1930s radio factory, has sadly been pushed aside by new, more central hotels on the block. Now business bores and furniture aficionados are enjoying

its *mezzo* positioning close to La Fiera. Agreeably linear (and peaceful), the four-star Enterprise is warmed up with *chinoiserie*: the lobby is a tall, functional space in cream marble and mahogany with a neat series of cosy zones with oriental antiques. Its striking Privé Bar (not really private, just intimate) is like a Buddhist shrine with a gold leaf dome, a green onyx backlit bar and 18th-century Asian antiques; the contemporary Sophia's Restaurant comes highly recommended. Its 109 rooms are what you'd expect of a minimalist design hotel, with pared down modern styling, giant suede headboards and shimmering Bisazza mosaic bathrooms. All are furnished with premium brands Flos and Cassina, gratifying for Fiera-bound *interioristas*.

Style 8, Atmosphere 7, Location 6

Excelsior Hotel Gallia, Piazza Duca D'Aosta, 9, Porta Venezia
Tel: 02 678 51   www.excelsiorgallia.it
Rates: €190–720

The Gallia, founded by Carlo Gallia in 1932, holds its own alongside the monumental Stazione Centrale with its own majestic Liberty-style façade and tomato-red canopies (an addition by current owner Le Méridien). A five-star hotel with 237 rooms and 15 suites, and a member of The Leading Hotels of the World group, the Gallia rests on its historic grandeur of handsome,

large public spaces, tall ceilings and antique chandeliers, and a beautiful central staircase with Liberty stained-glass windows. Now such glory has been muted by a faceless population of business travellers. Rooms are generously sized and traditionally decorated with period furniture; and all doubles have king-sized beds. Needless to say, all business needs are taken care of, and there's a restaurant, and exercise and beauty centres. During World War II it served as the German HQ for North Italy, and the occupying German general's nickname – the Baboon – has been appropriated for the Gallia's modern and cosy bar.

Style 8, Atmosphere 6, Location 7

Four Seasons Hotel, Via Gesù, 6, Centro
Tel: 02 770 88 www.fourseasons.com/milan
Rates: €627–1,210

Staying at the award-winning Four Seasons – which rose phoenix-like from the ashes of a 15th-century convent right in the centre of Fashion Central – commands considerable status. In a rare (and winning) mix of old and new, the Four Seasons has conserved the convent's few remaining frescos, columns and cloisters – visible in the Il Foyer piano bar (originally the chapel; now serving excellent and expensive Bloody Marys to Milan's power classes) and the quieter chianti-coloured library with a real fireplace. Two restaurants – Il Teatro (see Eat) and La Veranda, plus vast banqueting facilities (where affluent Milanese

host their wedding receptions), a fitness room and a picturesque courtyard garden should answer most needs. All 77 super-luxe rooms and 41 suites come with plasma TVs and DVD players, music systems (and compilation CDs), heated marble bathroom floors and steam-proof mirrors, and all guests are provided with complimentary mobile phones because the reception here is not always perfect. If all this doesn't satisfy, 'everything is possible' with the Four Seasons' famed six-star service (at high five-star prices).

Style 9, Atmosphere 8, Location 9

Grand Hotel et de Milan, Via Manzoni, 29, Centro
Tel: 02 723 141 www.grandhoteletdemilan.it
Rates: €280–770

Amid much competition for central five-star hotels, the Milan is the preferred choice for a veritable golden book of royalty, statesmen and stars past and present (its devotees drop the name's clumsy 'et de', a French wartime addition). Many of its 18 suites are dedicated to its historic guests, including Verdi, Callas and Nureyev (it's evidently handy for La Scala). Opened in 1863 and now a member of the Leading Hotels of the World, the superlatively refined Milan is unusual because it offers tradition with taste, backed up with discreet and earnest service. Behind a grand neo-Gothic façade, a further 77 well-sized rooms are individually decorated in Austro-Hungarian imperial style with grace-

ful repro and antique furniture, parquet floors, high ceilings and large marble bathrooms. Priceless European antiques adorn the public areas – namely the Falstaff bar and its two restaurants, the Caruso (with summer courtyard) and Don Carlos (with a Michelin-starred chef). The modern glass-cubed fitness centre is incongruously suspended in the courtyard like a goldfish bowl – useful for unsolicited star-spotting.

Style 9, Atmosphere 7, Location 9

Grand Hotel Duomo, Via San Raffaele, 1, Centro
Tel: 02 883 3 www.grandhotelduomo.com
Rates €350–950

Visitors to Milan with an ambition of waking up to a view of the Duomo should check into the Grand Hotel Duomo. All its suites and superior rooms come with a view (and a premium) since it flanks the Piazza del Duomo. The hotel also comes with tourist-pleasing history, as it is housed within the 19th-century Palazzo Mengoni, designed by eminent Milanese architect Giuseppe Mengoni who also designed the hotel's next-door neighbour, the Galleria Vittorio Emanuele II. This 162-room five-star hotel is now owned by the art-dealing Marabini family. Its interior has been decorated according to the contemporary taste of Liana, the wife, and while there is lots of colour and light, its look is slightly busy with add-on layers of renovation and artwork over the years. Guests are best off looking outwards at the excellent

views – from the first-floor Ristorante Duomo (somewhat past its sell-by date now) that looks out at the Duomo through a 19th-century portico, or from the large roof terrace serviced by the L'Orangerie restaurant; only committed tourists need stay for the meal.

Style 7, Atmosphere 7, Location 9

The Gray, Via San Raffaele, 6, Centro
Tel: 02 720 895   www.hotelthegray.com
Rates: €450–900

Designed by Guido Ciompi (architect of Gucci boutiques and Roberto Cavalli's house) with much pink, orange and red, there's very little that's grey about this super-central five-star design hotel. Its 21 rooms are individually decked out in the last word in fashionable furniture, DVD and CD players (plus the soft-ware), wenge wood, and chrome and glass Starck bathrooms. Guests can use the gym and pool of sister-hotel Hotel de la Ville, but it's much better to book into one of two of Gray's rooms with private gyms and concentrate on working it in their own exclusive amenities, namely 'Il Bar' and 'Le Noir', an all-black restaurant with tables on sliding rails for cosying up with the fashion fraternity, who pack in here during Fashion Week. Restricted numbers at the Gray is well suited for those needing to keep a low profile, and for going unnoticed on the foyer's fabulous hot pink Alice-in-Wonderland swing.

Hotel de la Ville, Via Hoepli, 6, Centro
Tel: 02 879 1311   www.delavillemilano.com
Rates: €194–710

Like a Sherlock Holmes film set, the four-star Hotel de la Ville verges on kitsch in the extent of its quaint Englishness. Possibly *de trop* for some tastes with heavy patterned carpets, dark damask walls, cherrywood panelling and silk tasselled brocade furniture, it's very popular with the Japanese and Americans, and not least because it's right in the zone (some of the 98 rooms face the Duomo). Unusually for Milan, it also has a rooftop swimming pool, and although skinny and shallow (not unusual in Milan), it's refreshingly modern and surrounded by a pleasing bamboo-walled garden, sunloungers and decking. In the summer, the roof is peeled back, and residents can take cocktails in a bikini under the Duomo. Its low-ceilinged lounge bar, Il Visconteo, harks right back to Holmes with Stubbs-style equestrian art and a private (and now full) cigar club complete with 24 brass-plaqued private humidors. The fitness club and L'Opera restaurant are more elementary, dear readers.

Hotel dei Cavalieri, Piazza Missori, 1, Centro
Tel: 02 885 71 www.hoteldeicavalieri.com
Rates: €209–900

In a horseshoe-shaped building that abuts Piazza Missori and its
equestrian statue, having opened in 1949 on the site of a 19th-
century inn and stables for cavaliers, the four-star Hotel dei
Cavalieri has something of a horsey theme. It also has a little-
known design pedigree, with a striking 1950s wooden-panelled
lobby designed by Gio Ponti (he also designed the ninth floor,
where the hotel's largest rooms can be found). Recently renovated, the lobby and bar are now stylishly fitted with chunky black
leather sofas and a black stone floor, giving it a modern gentlemen's club feel. On the 10th floor is a roof terrace from where
the San Siro football stadium can be seen on a clear day, with a
restaurant and bar that are open in the summer. The first-floor
restaurant is open all year. With quadruple glazing in the 200
rooms and four suites, it's easy to forget the central location of
this thoroughbred hotel.

Style 8, Atmosphere 7, Location 8

Hotel Mediolanum, Via M Macchi, 1, Porta Venezia
Tel: 02 670 5312 www.mediolanumhotel.com
Rates: €115–500

45

Named after the Latin name for Milan, the four-star Hotel Mediolanum is certainly historic, although its reference is much more contemporary: the 1970s. A sympathetic refurbishment in 2003 has transformed a drab '70s tower into a fashionable design hotel. The 51 unusual rooms in loud colour schemes of avocado, salmon pink, sky blue and deep orange still feature the original furniture and fittings, such as beige Formica tables and twiddly built-in radios; wallpapers are tastefully stripy or geometric. Modern additions make it popular with business, leisure and fashion visitors, despite its unremarkable location. The walnut-panelled lobby, packed with requisite iconic pieces by Man Ray, B&B Italia and Cassina, seems a little contrived, although its modern retro space-age bar has more appeal. It shares its sister hotel's beautifully brick vaulted exercise room, 300m away and has its own restaurant and modest business booth.

Style 8, Atmosphere 7, Location 7

Hotel Principe di Savoia, Piazza della Repubblica, 17, Porta Venezia
Tel: 02 623 01 www.hotelprincipedisavoia.com
Rates: €440–3,116

Since it's owned by the Sultan of Brunei, it comes as no surprise that the design philosophy for the Principe is 'more is more'. It calls itself the *grande dame* of Milan's hotels, and with 278 rooms and 126 suites it takes the gold for size – and indeed for volume of gilt in the extravagant ground floor with its turn-of-the-century 'eclecticism' (the hotel was built in 1863). You don't get many square metres for your euro, but certainly the fuss doesn't stop at the bedroom door: soundproofed rooms are busy with opulent furni-

ture, rich damask walls and wood panelling. There's often a swarm of police outside: that's because VVIPS – including HRH Queen Elizabeth, George Bush and Michael Jackson – like to take the Principe's presidential suite for its bodyguard facilities (although the private swimming pool might have something to do with it). There's also an indoor pool for *hoi polloi* in the hotel gym (impressive enough to be a stand-alone gym), plus a piano bar, a rococo-style café and a gilded restaurant; it is also a member of the Leading Hotels of the World. Its massive conference set-up means that it is popular with business clients. In fact everything about the five-star Principe is super-sized, even down to the free stretched Mercedes service every 15 minutes to the *quadrilatero d'oro*, and this review.

Style 8, Atmosphere 8, Location 7

Hotel Sanpi, Via L Palazzi, 18, Porta Venezia
Tel: 02 295 133 41 www.hotelsanpimilano.it
Rates: €119–315

The lesser-known family-run Sanpi Hotel (named after Sandro and Piera, grandparents of present owner Alberto Bulgheroni) was built around a 19th-century railway signaller's house. This small and cheery villa – situated in the middle of a pretty courtyard garden – houses four of the hotel's 79 rooms, all snug with cottagey sprig-print linens. There are plenty of other eccentricities to this four-star hotel, which at first seems unexceptional, located in an urban wilderness near Buenos Aires. The décor is certainly 'eclectic' (chosen by Alberto's architect wife) and the common areas feature juxtaposed contemporary and period styles. Its rooms and six suites are thankfully either/or: the newly renovated wing features quirky modern furniture and colourful Alessi bathrooms (all connected by dark, starry and glittery corridors). Other rooms are classical in style with Regency stripes and floral upholstery. The 19th-century brick-vaulted ex-wine cellar fitness centre (which it shares with sister hotel Mediolanum), a tiny speakeasy-style bar and flowery breakfast room complete the idiosyncratic Sanpi.

Style 7, Atmosphere 7, Location 7

Hotel Spadari, Via Spadari, 11, Centro
Tel: 02 720 023 71 www.spadarihotel.com
Rates: €208–368

Open since 1991, the Spadari claimed the crown of Milan's first design hotel. More recently it has segued into an art hotel and pays Saatchi-like homage to emerging young artists. On a par subjectively but minus the sensation, the Spadari's collection of modern art, as commissioned and curated by Palazzo Reale's artistic director, adorns its 40 well-sized rooms, small lobby and breakfast room/bar, alongside contemporary European furniture. Pale carved wood by respected Italian artist Ugo La Pietra and a pale blue colour scheme (both apparently relaxing in chromatherapy terms) are used throughout the hotel. And with free bedtime storybooks laid out like goodnight chocolates, and con-

certedly friendly service, the low-key family-run Spadari is unusual for creating calm right on the doorstep of the Duomo. It's also next door to Peck delicatessen (see Shop), but with all-day *pasticcini* from Milan's champion baker Ernest Knam, guests may prefer to indulge in pastries in peace here.

Style 7, Atmosphere 8, Location 8

Hotel Straf, Via San Raffaele, 3, Centro
Tel: 02 805 081   www.straf.it
Rates: €195–750

Your grandmother would probably dismiss the Straf as a building site. But the Straf is a four-star design hotel, no less, and a pioneer of the rather extreme 'unfinished industrial' look, with distressed cement walls, scratched mirrors, and burnished copper panels. It opened in winter 2003 in a 19th-century neo-Renaissance building next to the Duomo, although no such historic influences are at play here – this is pure forward-looking minimalist design. Public spaces are certainly rather minimal – with an austere foyer, a breakfast room (a monochrome cube),

and Straf bar (a concrete cube), which makes for mild claustro-phobia since it's right on the tourist zone's frontline. But the cachet of staying at the Straf more than makes up for that for its hip fan base of professional creatives, who fill out its 66 unique rooms, all with designer bathrooms, flat-screen TV and music systems, exposed concrete and builders' scrawlings.

Style 9, Atmosphere 7, Location 9

Park Hyatt Milano, Via T Grossi, 1, Centro
Tel: 02 882 112 34 www.milan.park.hyatt.com
Rates: €450–3,200

Among a new breed of haute hotels is the modern-classic Park Hyatt Milano, designed in the pure, clean lines of American archi-tect Ed Tuttle and open since winter 2003. Positioned practically inside the Galleria Vittorio Emanuele II in the shell of an 1875 palazzo, the five-star Park Hyatt has views of both the Duomo and the Galleria (you can practically window-shop at Prada from your bed). Inside is a veritable study in Roman travertine stone, with 18,000m^2 of the creamy rock all over the hotel, concentrat-ed in a dramatic circular foyer with a soaring glass dome (mod-elled on the Galleria's). There's a fitness centre, spa and restau-rant, and The Park Bar, one of few hotel bars – in restrained shades of grey, aubergine and black – to attract Milan's style cognoscenti for *aperitivo*. Big spenders check straight into one of the 117 capacious rooms and suites with bathroom-sized show-

ers, B&O TVs and CD players and fresh fruit platters delivered
daily. Service is professional and friendly, but if there's a solemn
atmosphere, it's because, while some are here to spend, most are
here to make big bucks in nearby Piazza Affari.

Style 9, Atmosphere 7, Location 9

Petit Palais, Via Molino delle Armi, 1, Navigli
Tel: 02 584 891   www.petitpalais.it
Rates: €175–440

The Petit Palais is more accurately a *piccolo palazzo*, but the family owners thought it sounded more alluring in French. Its *salotto*
– or drawing room – which serves as the lobby, is perfectly
enticing with Venetian and Florentine antiques, Murano chandeliers, pistachio silk curtains, an ornate fireplace and family

photographs – the expensive clutter of a typical Lombardy palazzo. The reception is like a nobleman's bureau with its grand green leather antique writing table. The rooms are more repro than real, but with Fortuny upholstery, monogrammed Frette bedlinen and towels, Etro toiletries and fresh flowers, guests can still entertain a fantasy of aristocratic connections. With just 18 suites split between four-star hotel accommodation and longer-term residency, it's cosy and intimate, and the service is friendly and personalized (a 24-hour porter takes care of matters after hours). Straddling the Centro and Navigli, Petit Palais is near everything but nothing in particular: what better excuse to take a cognac in front of the fireplace?

> **Style 8, Atmosphere 8, Location 8**

Sheraton Diana Majestic, Viale Piave 42, Porta Venezia
Tel: 02 205 81 www.sheraton.com/DianaMajestic
Rates: €405–1,010

The Milanese revere the Diana for its glorious Liberty façade (from 1908) and its elite Diana Garden bar (see Drink). The bar overlooks the hotel's delightful gardens, which contain the statue of the Roman goddess Diana from which the takes its name. But the Diana's rooms and corridors lack such grandeur, despite conservative renovations that have included modest business facilities and a fitness room. However, its old-style charm means that all 107 rooms and suites are different, decorated in a classical

imperial style in soft, earthy colours with large marble bathrooms. Modern touches include Bose CD players in every room, and a rather mean automated minibar – just pick up that *premier cru* and you'll be charged for it. The best rooms are those with a view of the garden – the biggest selling point of this four-star hotel.

Style 7, Atmosphere 8, Location 8

Townhouse 31, Via Goldoni 31, Porta Venezia
Tel: 02 701 56 www.townhouse.it
Rates: €240–450

The design brief of Townhouse 31 (named after its street number, not the room count – it has just 17) is 'at home with a well-travelled sophisticate'. Entry is through a Chinese pergola and a baroque outdoor bar; the lobby is more relaxed with deep cream sofas, parquet floor and eclectic ethnic furnishings from Morocco, Africa and the Orient. The four-star Townhouse – the first in a chain of family-run boutique hotels (also Townhouse 12, Piazza Gerusalemme, 12; tel: 02 890 785 12; and Townhouse Duomo, opening beginning 2006) – does not have the facilities of a large hotel, but its 24-hour hotel butler can prepare meals (there's no restaurant here) and oblige most demands; laptops and mobile phones are available on request. The owners, who live next door, have been known to shuttle guests around when taxis are unavailable. Rooms are simple and low-key (and

expensive for what they are); all include plasma TVs, linen sheets and aromatherapy pillows. Its exclusive bed-and-breakfast feel is most apparent at the communal breakfast table – a revolution in bleak hotel breakfasts.

Style 8, Atmosphere 8/9, Location 7

UNA Hotel Tocq, Via A de Tocqueville, 7/D, Garibaldi
Tel: 02 620 71 www.unahotels.it
Rates: €163–450

The Tocq, one of five Italian UNA hotels in Milan, is their four-star 'boutique' offering. In reality it is a boutique-business hotel: opened in 1998 near the business district of Porta Garibaldi and the nightlife of Corso Como, it's aimed at the work-hard/play-hard crowd. The contemporary lobby and bar have Schrager aspirations, decked out in travertine stone, beech wood, glass walls and *objets d'art*. The large ground-floor bar, with its coloured neon-lit zones, imposing stainless-steel food island and central glass stairs (that lead up to the restaurant) is evidently

hoping to compete with Corso Como's finest. But behind the façade, the 122 light and minimalist rooms are more Ikea than Le Corbusier, with beech furniture and panelling, beige furnishings and white bed linen. Business facilities aplenty don't deter the Italian footballers who pile in on Sunday evenings after the game to take advantage of its tripping distance to and from the clubs.

The Westin Palace, Piazza della Repubblica, 20, Porta Venezia
Tel: 02 633 61 www.westin.com/palacemilan
Rates: €270–1,510

With its king-sized lobby of dazzling chandeliers, neo-classical gilt cornicing and mirrored columns, you'd be forgiven for thinking you'd walked into an Arabian palace rather than the five-star Westin Palace. Now owned by American chain Starwood, it was bombed to bits in World War II and completely rebuilt in 1950 as a marble-clad modern towerblock. No such mediocrity inside – this is an elaborate reworking of Italian Renaissance architecture and all its excesses. Its 241 rooms and 16 suites (10 with private Turkish baths) are all finished in a colourful imperial style with antique and repro 19th-century furniture, and fitted with Westin's Heavenly beds (supposedly an 'unforgettable sleeping experience'); the roof terrace restaurant affords city views in the summer. The opulent ground-floor lounge bar, with a marble colonnade and tropical water fountain, lures the arrivistes; Starwood's loyalty scheme and ample convention facilities draws in the corporate clients.

eat...

It's no surprise that fashion exerts a huge influence on food in Milan and its most important restaurants are equally fashion- and foodie-orientated – style versus substance, often mutually exclusive. But eating is not the most important thing to the style mafia: it's more about seeing and being seen (notice the proliferation of mirrors in restaurants for inward-sitting folk to check their rear view). And as is the nature of fashion, fast trends die young: just as soon as new restaurants become the flavour of the month, they can just as quickly fall out of favour again. Milan's fashion restaurants with promise of staying-power and a bridge to good food are Eda, Altro Spazio Strato, Milch, Quattrocento and Noy.

Milan shares a nationwide pride in its cuisine, and believes that the Italian way is the best way – food is usually quite purist (for example, Italians believe that the only point of a creamy sauce is to conceal poor ingredients). Certainly, there's an excellent standard of ingredients available in Milan (be sure to indulge in the white truffle season – between mid-November and mid-January). Generally Italians are happiest eating and drinking Italian produce; international wine lists really only exist for tourists. The Milanese are very proud of their traditional dishes – most places offer *ossobucco* (veal shank), *risotto alla milanese* (with saffron and bone marrow) and *cotoletta* (veal cutlet). Leaning on the stodgy side,

these dishes may not be to everyone's taste and there are plenty restaurants that specialize in other regions of Italy. Highly recommended are Xe Mauri (Venetian), Giulio Pane e Ojo (Roman), 13 Giugno and Da Giacomo (both Sicilian). A handful of Milan's restaurants have been rewarded with Michelin stars, namely Aimo e Nadia with one star, and Cracco-Peck and Sadler with two.

Cosmopolites are welcoming the rise of international imports, although these are often a very sanitized version of the original. The Milanese worry about the hygiene standards of foreign kitchens so for an ethnic restaurant to work, there's an assumption that it needs to be presented as a theme restaurant, often ending up rather over-the-top and artificial; strong tastes are often diluted and the food can be insipid. However, the Milanese do understand Japanese food (Low in fat! High in design! So cosmopolitan!), so it's easy to get good sushi here. Our favourite ethnic restaurants are Finger's (Japanese), Shambala (Thai/Vietnamese) and Don Juan (Argentine).

Milanese xenophobia extends to service and there's a prevailing prejudice – especially in the more traditional establishments – that foreigners are ignorant about food (especially the English because they apparently put up with such terrible cooking). A virtually nonexistent tipping culture offers Milan's waiters little incentive to remember their manners, and tourists are given short shrift in any case because they are not expected to return. Fashion restaurants are generally much more tuned in to an international set, but even in informal restaurants, no waiter will stomach downbeat dressing. It's usual for chefs to roam the floor to meet and greet and accept compliments.

Booking is essential for any restaurant in Milan, especially at rush hour (from 9pm, but later in the summer). Most restaurants close for much of August and many for two weeks from Christmas to Epiphany (6 January).

Restaurants are rated in three categories: food (quality of ingredients, cooking and presentation), service (efficiency and warmth) and atmosphere. The price is calculated on the cost of three courses for one, half a bottle of wine and the ubiquitous cover charge (up to €5).

Our top ten restaurants in Milan are:
1. Cracco-Peck
2. Il Luogo di Aimo e Nadia
3. Finger's
4. Altro Spazio Strato
5. Quattrocento
6. Sadler
7. Il Teatro
8. Xe Mauri
9. Boccondivino
10. Controvapore

Our top five restaurants for food are:
1. Cracco-Peck
2. Il Luogo di Aimo e Nadia
3. Sadler
4. Il Teatro
5. Joia

Our top five restaurants for service are:
1. Boccondivino
2. Tano Passimi l'Olio
3. Controvapore
4. Shambala
5. Bussarakham

Our top five restaurants for atmosphere are:
1. Trattoria Toscana
2. Giulio Pane e Ojo
3. Xe Mauri
4. Quattrocento
5. Eda

13 Giugno, Via Goldoni, 44, Porta Venezia
Tel: 02 719 654 www.ristorante13giugno.it
Open: 12.30–2.30pm, 8–11.30pm. Closed Sundays, last three
weeks of August and first week of January.   €80

Courting couples looking for aphrodisiacs might get lucky at
Tredici Giugno. Not only does this Sicilian seafood restaurant
serve oysters by the bucket, but in the enchanting surroundings
of soft lighting, polished wooden furniture and leafy corners, a
pianist sings famous Italian love songs. Failing that, charm your
date with the story of the restaurant, which was dedicated to
the owner's father – who was born on 13 June 1913 and
spawned 13 children. Saverio, his youngest, opened 13 Giugno in
1986; his English wife Barbara now runs their second branch in
Brera (Piazza Mirabello, 1; tel: 02 290 033 00). Saverio and chef
Damiano are both Sicilian, so expect hearty servings of unfussy
fish dishes complemented by a Sicilian wine list and Milan's best-
looking grappa trolley. Ever the host, the jovial Saverio serenades
the restaurant with ballads; play your ace by making a request.

Food 8, Service 8, Atmosphere 8

360°, Via Tortona, 12, Navigli
Tel: 02 835 6706
Open: 12.30–4pm Tues–Sun, 8pm–midnight Thurs–Sat.
Closed between Christmas and Epiphany, and last three
weeks of August.   €50

Design friends Monica and Angelo dreamt respectively of opening a restaurant and a Madagascan plant shop. In 2000, they joined forces to build an oasis of healthy wholefoods in a fresh environment. They called it 360° because it would encompass all sorts: in this ex-shutter factory they also exhibit art and have a Shiatsu/Thai massage room (advance booking necessary). The vibe is laid-back and laissez-faire, with an ethnic-influenced buffet of salads, curries and spicy vegetables. Fashionably 1970s in style, it resembles a camp canteen for a progressive secondary school, with beige stacking chairs, psychedelic tablecloths and pink and orange walls. It attracts a fashionable crowd, not least since Via Tortona is full of design and photographic studios. In fact it's so fashionable that major league fashion designers often hold private parties here so call ahead to check.

Food 7, Service 7, Atmosphere 8

Alla Cucina delle Langhe, Corso Como, 6, Garibaldi
Tel: 02 655 4279
Open: 12.30–2.30pm, 7.30–11.15pm. Closed Sundays,
and August.   €55

Le Langhe is Tom Ford's favourite restaurant in Milan – when at Gucci, he would reserve a table here for the whole of Milan Fashion Week. It is certainly the best restaurant on Corso

Como, and a favourite because of the surrounding nightlife.
There's a good upbeat vibe from spirited party-goers, including
carb-loading footballers and international models with their PRs,
in the informal *insalateria* upstairs – although celebrities are
treated like normal people in this unpretentious trattoria.
Likewise, fleeting fashions are ignored: the décor is reolutely

retro with William Morris-style floral wallpaper, Folies Bergères
posters, and in the ground-floor conservatory, a rare framed collection of Mussolini's fascist art magazine *La Rivista*. The name
'Langhe' is in fact a region in Piedmont, and Papi, chef of 17
years, produces competent Piedmontese specialities, to be
washed down with regional wines. Take a tip from Tom Ford: his
favourite is *fusilli alle herbe*.

Food 8, Service 8, Atmosphere 8

Altro Spazio Strato, Via F Burlamacchi, 5, Porta Romana
Tel: 02 541 218 04   www.t-altro.com
Open: midday–3pm, 8pm–midnight. Closed Mon lunch, Sun and
first three weeks of August.   €90

Altro (or 'other') is the new concept restaurant attached to
deluxe interiors emporium Spazio Strato. Dining here is amidst
the extreme sophistication of Strato furniture and Strato architecture; even the *bagni* are showrooms. Strato style is sharp and

angular, ordered and spacious – thus, modern retro furniture is geometrically arranged within two large dining rooms (or glass cubes lined with wenge wood and cappuccino stone flooring). Paris-trained head chef Fabrizio Ferrari can be observed through a glass screen preparing innovative gourmet dishes with French-inspired sauces, which come as a rare yet welcome embellishment in Milan. The wine cellar is pan-Italian with some international labels for tourists – with an annual invasion of furniture-fair-goers, Altro is internationally attuned and service is warm and attentive. And of course all the interiors are available to buy – ordering off-menu never was so pricey (although staying on-menu doesn't come cheap).

Food 8, Service 9, Atmosphere 7

Antica Trattoria della Pesa, Viale Pasubio, 10, Garibaldi
Tel: 02 655 5741
Open: 12.30–2.30pm, 7.30–11pm. Closed Sundays and
throughout August.   €70

For *tipico* Milanese food, locals and tourists pile into the historic Antica Trattoria della Pesa, unchanged since opening in 1880. It takes its name from the now-disused weighbridge (*pesa*) on its doorstep, where merchants' goods would be weighed on entering or leaving the city (when indeed this was the edge of the city). Departing diners will be thankful that the scales cannot gauge their extra weight. Bestsellers include *ossobucco*, *risotto alla milanese* and *costaletta* (here spelled the traditional way, not the apparently wrong way, *cotaletta*). At Christmas time, *panettone* from Gattullo (see Snack) comes smothered in *zabaione*. And every time regulars Giorgio Armani and Carla Sozzani come for dinner, they take the *risotto al salto* (traditional Milanese risotto that's pan-fried and crispy, and not so easy to find). Don't be tempted by non-traditional dishes like curry – plump for the classics.

Food 8, Service 7, Atmosphere 7

Armani/Nobu, Via Pisoni, 1, Centro
Tel: 02 723 186 45 www.giorgioarmani.com
Open: midday–2.30pm Tues–Fri, 7pm–midnight Mon–Sat. Closed
Sundays.   €85

Since Nobu is arguably the Armani of sushi – understated and expensive trophies of design – it was smart of Giorgio Armani and Nobu founder Nobuyuki Matsuhisa to collaborate by open-ing a branch in Milan. Although not as acclaimed as its sister restaurant in London, the food is cheaper and the atmosphere more casual. Classics such as black cod and caviar in Nobu 'new-style' (with Californian and South American influences) are served up by waiters who work with the impersonal speed and service of a sushi conveyor belt. Located on the first floor of Armani's 'superstore', it is decked out in Japanese-inspired Armani Casa décor. With orange upholstery and matching lighting, it's rather like a first-class Easyjet departure lounge. The international crowd matches the food – good-looking and light-

weight; black-clad fashionistas and status-seekers doing face time offer excellent social anthropological opportunities. Financially challenged civilians could watch the parade from the ground-floor lounge bar where Nobu *maki* is presented with *aperitivo*.

Food 7, Service 6, Atmosphere 7

Bagutta, Via Bagutta, 14, Centro
Tel: 02 760 009 02   www.bagutta.it
Open: 12.30–2.30pm, 7.30–10.30pm. Closed Sundays, last three weeks of August, and two weeks at Christmas.   €65

Bagutta is a hall of fame of Milan's 20th-century literati. Bagutta has its own story to tell (and even has its own *libretto*)… Once upon a time in 1924 Alberto Pepori opened a cheap trattoria. It became a rendezvous for impoverished writers who decided to fine each other for being late or absent; the funds would be given to their favourite writer. The esteemed Premio Bagutta (Bagutta prize) has been awarded every year since (although now it is sponsored by a bank). And less a cheap trattoria now than a mid-range restaurant seating 200 (and 180 more in the summer garden), it serves a wide choice of traditional Italian fare to habitués and tourists alike. It's worth seeing for just what the Peporis call a free art gallery – every wall is covered in historical caricatures of 'Baguttiani' (prize-winners) and judges. This story seems set to run and run.

Food 7, Service 8, Atmosphere 8

Boccondivino, Via Carducci, 17, Navigli
Tel: 02 866 040 www.boccondivino.com
Open: 8pm–midnight. Closed Sundays and first three weeks of
August.   €70

Boccondivino – a play on words meaning 'divine mouthful' or 'mouthful of wine' – is something of an understatement. It's more like eight courses' worth. There's no menu and no choice – leave picky eaters behind, loosen your belt and enjoy a *degustazione* of traditional Italian food. The running order, unchanged since the restaurant opened in 1976, starts with *prosecco* and *aperitivo*, followed by crudités, two *salami* courses (don't shrink away from the *lardo*: just one mouthful is actually divine), the requisite carbohydrate course, and two rounds of seasonal cheeses, rounded off with *biscotti* and sorbet. Each is matched with an appropriate wine from a cellar with more than 900 Italian labels, and by the end of the meal you'll be surrounded by enough glasses to play an entire octave of glass-notes. Service is entertaining and educational (and multi-lingual). The setting is like a glorified college hall, with vaulted brick ceilings, whitewashed walls and long dining tables spread over three rooms, and chances are you'll acquire some new dining companions on the communal tables.

Food 8, Service 9, Atmosphere 8

Boeucc, Piazza Belgioioso, 2, Centro
Tel: 02 760 202 24 www.boeucc.com
Open: 12.30–2.30pm, 8–10.30pm. Closed Sun lunch and Sat. €75

Boeucc (pronounced 'birch') is old Milanese slang for 'hole'. When it opened back in 1696 (it claims the title of Milan's first restaurant), it was indeed hole-sized. Now this archetypal *antico ristorante* occupies a large 18th-century hall (originally horses' stables) with granite columns, vaulted ceilings and oak panelling that is tucked away in a secluded courtyard shared with novelist Alessandro Manzoni's historic house. The menu is accordingly traditional, with Roman, Florentine and Milanese influences: *saltimbocca*, *ossobucco*, *cotaletta* and *risotto alla milanese*, all pre-pared by Piero Berzelo, chef of 25 years. With such heavyweight classics, and any notion of need knocked out with canapés and *petits fours*, dining here can be a gluttonous experience. Needless to say its history is coloured with the names of nobility and (operatic) royalty; now it is popular among affluent Milanese families and foreign business clients. Black bow-tied waiters provide a seamless if rather formal service, with a fittingly Italian insistence on cash payment (or Amex).

Food 8, Service 8, Atmosphere 6

Bussarakham, Via Valenza, 13, Navigli
Tel: 02 894 224 15
Open: midday–2.30pm, 7.45–11.15pm. Closed Mon/Tue lunch and throughout August.   €55

For an ethnic restaurant to succeed in Milan, it needs five-star gloss. Thai restaurant Bussarakham (meaning 'topaz') has left nothing to chance, opening in spring 2004 as a sumptuous wooden palace filled with ornately carved teak furniture, tropical palms and orchids, gold fabrics and stencilled walls, and oriental waitresses who bow on your arrival, promptly deliver prawn crackers, and attend to whims like first-class air-hostesses. The food is surprisingly undiluted with kicking curries and authentic flavours, all garnished with exotic flowers and served on traditional mint green varnished ceramics. Seating 100, it's good for groups, and with lots of carved wooden partitions and strategic foliage, can also be romantic and tranquil; the soundtrack swings between Buddha Bar lounge music and traditional Thai love songs. Upstairs is a cute beach-hut-style room where diners hunker down on triangular mats at low tables with recessed

footwells; here the Milanese are likely to leave veteran backpackers to it.

Chandelier, Via Broggi, 17, Porta Venezia
Tel: 02 202 404 58   www.chandelier.it
Open: 6.30pm–2am (kitchen 8pm–12.30am). Closed Mondays
and throughout August.   €90

The name seems pretty obvious once ensconced in this Aladdin's
cave of resplendent baroque décor. Crystal chandeliers are ubiquitous in Milan but Chandelier wins the crown of one-upmanship
with this outrageous temple of overstatement: rows of flickering
chandeliers and candelabras, sweeping Swarovski crystal curtains,
vast gilt thrones adorned with cherubs, and enough mirrors to
satisfy the neediest of narcissists. If you can't take the visual
assault, there is a cooler green zone; if you want it all, you can –
from its pricey store, 'Chandelier Charm', just up the street (all
is designed by owner and interior designer Antonio Coppola).
Fashionable showfood, with wanton ingredients such as foïe gras
and champagne, complements a modern Italian menu; reassuring-
ly cool waiters behave as if they would rather be elsewhere. Its
critics would too – and it is a case of love it or loathe it – they
say overpriced, underwhelmed. We say go with a sense of
humour – and a tiara.

Food 7, Service 7, Atmosphere 8

Chatulle, Via Piero della Francesca, 68, Parco Sempione
Tel: 02 342 008 www.chatulle.it
Open: 11.30am–3pm, 7pm–3am. Closed Sat/Sun lunch and
throughout August.   €55

Chatulle is rather heaven-like with its all-cream interior of arches, diaphanous floor-length curtains, padded leather seating,
bleached oak tables, limestone floor tiles and a dazzlingly sparkly
crystal chandelier that stretches the length of the bar. If you're
having an ugly day, you might also feel you've found heaven since
Chatulle artfully flatters one's features with indirect lighting, soft

candlelight and warm reflective tones. And with a plentiful supply of gratuitous mirrors, it gently indulges the Milanese vanities. The menu – of traditional Italian and Milanese dishes with meat-heavy main courses – seems suspiciously Atkins-orientated, but portions are generous and good value, and service is efficient and obliging; the bar offers *aperitivo* and an opportunity for late post-dinner drinking. It's a fashionable place to fill up at, in this out-of-the-way street that's filling up with nightlife (including its sister club Gattopardo; see Party).

Food 8, Service 8, Atmosphere 7

Cigair, Via Molino Delle Armi, 25, Navigli
Tel: 02 8942 0089   www.cigair.it
Open: 8pm–1am daily   €60

Milan's cigar aficionados congregate at Cigair, previously a members-only club and now open to all cigar-lovers (non-smokers are tolerated). A shrine to the hallowed Havana cigar, this former car workshop still with original hoists is bedecked with cigar memorabilia: even the lavatories are labelled Romeo and Julietta; the smiling, smoking Groucho Marx serves as their mascot. The walk-in humidor is the largest in Europe with a shop stocked with rare Montecristos and Cohibas, a members' lounge and a members' storage vault (for the likes of Pavarotti and owner Andrea Molinari). The food – simple but good-quality Italian – is

evidently secondary here, but juicy butch steaks particularly complement a cigar-touting *machismo*. Live bands perform on Tuesdays, Thursdays and Saturdays, there's *al fresco* seating in the summer, and the Cuban barman servicing the long 1950s Miami-style bar and lounge makes the best Mojitos in Milan.

Food 7, Service 8, Atmosphere 8

Compagnia Generale dei Viaggiatori Naviganti e Sognatori, Via Cuccagna, 4, Porta Romana
Tel: 02 551 6154
Open: 8–11.30pm. Closed Mondays and last three weeks of August.   €65

Such a title deserves an explanation – and an abbreviation. Compagnia Generale (aka the Society of Travellers, Navigators and Dreamers, aka Trattoria Giapponese) started out as a sailing club, founded in 1986 by current owner and sailor Cosimo Vezzoni (evidently, sailing is but a dream in Milan). In 1995, he and his wife Antonella transformed it into a Japanese trattoria – sushi in a relaxed Italian style. Set in a private, forgotten street of 18th-century peasant houses, this elegant farmhouse with exposed brick vaults and intimate lighting is furnished with a fusion of modern Italian and traditional Japanese décor. Of the three dining rooms, the best ambience is at the *tatami*, where shoes are removed and Japanese *geta* sandals are provided. The

footprint of original sushi chef Roberto Okabe (now at Finger's restaurant) lives on in the sushi, sashimi, tempura, teppanyaki and noodle dishes and rich desserts by champion pastry chef Ernest Knam, and keeps the glamorati coming back for more.

Food 7, Service 8, Atmosphere 8

Controvapore, Via C Goldoni, 3, Porta Venezia
Tel: 02 763 906 36
Open: 8.30–11pm daily   €85

Controvapore is a love story in catering. Cristina and Alessandro Mantovani met in 1997 and decided to pool resources to pursue their dream together. In 1999 they opened Controvapore, a veritable love nest, an intimate, plum-red candlelit space with seven antique tables. Appropriately, this quiet and mellow hideaway with no street sign is ideal for trysts; guests must knock for entry. Regulars request the *troni*, two 19th-century Genoan thrones around an antique Piedmontese table worth €10,000. For added privacy (and a premium of €25 per person), the new *salon privé* has just three tables, decorated with Bohemian crystal glass, real silver cutlery and antique Umbrian linen. All the aesthetics are taken care of by Alessandro, a one-time antiques dealer, and Cristina provides a very personal service, patiently translating the handwritten menu of Tuscan, Umbrian and Sicilian cuisine, while Alessandro's mother prepares Controvapore's specialities: tender Tuscan *chianina* beef and sublimely fresh pasta; rare

vintage wines are matched to taste.

Food 8, Service 9, Atmosphere 8

Cracco-Peck, Via Victor Hugò, 4, Centro
Tel: 02 876 774 www.peck.it
Open: 12.30–2.30pm, 7.30–10pm. Closed Sat lunch,
Sun and last three weeks of August.   €120

For exemplary *alta cucina*, most Milanese would call first at
Cracco-Peck. This two Michelin-starred restaurant opened in
2001 as a gastronomic showcase for Milan's premier delicatessen,
Peck. Head chef Carlo Cracco conjures up traditional Italian cuisine with a contemporary twist, made with the finest ingredients
– all available at the shop (Via Spadari, 9) should you be feeling

supremely confident. The exhaustive wine list from the shop's
exceptional wine cellar with more than 5,000 labels reads like the
Never-ending Story. In a sleek, coolly modern environment of linear
Japanese-style cherrywood panelling, frequented by power bro-
kers and plutocrats, best behaviour is imperative (not least for
the all-seeing dour waiters in formal black suits). A more relaxed
crowd eating more casual (and slightly cheaper) fare made with
the same superlative ingredients can be found next door at the
new Peck Italian Bar, Via Cantù, 3 (tel: 02 869 3017).

Food 10, Service 8, Atmosphere 7

Da Bice, Via Borgospesso, 12, Centro
Tel: 02 760 025 72 www.bicemilano.it
Open: 12.30–2.30pm, 7.30–22.45pm. Closed Sunday.   €70

Ask any Milanese local for restaurant recommendations and Da Bice always features. Da Bice has stuck to what it does best through three generations: simple, traditional Italian food with no surprises. Da Bice is also known for its famous clientele: super-models and Hollywood actors invariably refuel here when shopping in the *quadrilatero d'oro.* Opened in 1926 by a Tuscan restaurateur called Bice (short for Beatrice), it was taken over by her son Raymond who then handed it over to his daughters Roberta and Beatrice (Beatrice's husband Vincenzo is the chef). Milanese recipes (*ossobucco, risotto alla milanese*) have been added to the original Tuscan ones (*ribollita, pappardelle*) over time. Four quaint rooms are decorated with 1950s frescoes of Milan, wooden panelling and red tartan carpets. Top table is the 'family' table right by the kitchen, but if Naomi's in town you won't stand a chance.

Food 7, Service 7, Atmosphere 8

Da Giacomo, Via Sottocorno, 6, Porta Venezia
Tel: 02 760 233 13 www.dagiacomoristorante.it
Open: 12.30–2.30pm, 7.30–11pm. Closed Tues lunch
and Mon.   €60

Hovering somewhere between traditional and trendy, the family-run Da Giacomo has been a popular destination for moneyed Milanese – from the fashion industry to finance to family money – for over a decade. Designed by the late Renzo Mongiardino (the bourgeoisie's favourite interior designer), its classical elegance is remarkable. Two light, custard-coloured rooms with delicately stuccoed mint panels and pretty cornicing are adorned with art-deco lamps, antique racks of wine, lush foliage and still lifes of food. The food is resolutely unpretentious and always starts with a messy slice of sardine and caper pizza. It is known best for serving up ample portions of Sicilian fish, all cooked by

Giacomo's son-in-law Marco Monti; the shellfish comes particularly recommended. Service is erratic, but there's always Mongiardino's décor – or the clientele – to study while waiting.

Food 8, Service 7, Atmosphere 8

Dar el Yacout, Via Cadore, 23, Porta Romana
Tel: 02 546 2230 www.darelyacout.it
Open: 5pm–midnight daily. Closed August.   70€

Take some sequined belly dancers, add exotic drummers and singers, summon a retinue of fez-hatted, *babouche*-soled waiters laden with *tagines* of couscous and silver pots of mint tea, scatter rose petals liberally about a gold mosaic floor and finish with a puff on the hookah – and there you have a Vegas-quality

Moroccan themed restaurant. Opened in winter 2004, Dar el Yacout (meaning 'house of gold') took four years to build – it now stands as a Moroccan paradise on three floors thematically filled with eight-point stars, waterfalls, lanterns, stained glass, intricately carved furniture and rose incense. Unless you specify, you'll be ushered into a ceremonial six-course set menu on the ground floor where the waiters have been known to lose count of how many courses have been delivered, although this is the best spot to view the belly dancing on a central glass-covered aquamarine fountain. A la carte is available on the first floor (the second floor is a *salon privé* and cigar club).

Food 7, Service 7, Atmosphere 7

Don Juan, Via Altaguardia, 2, Porta Romana
Tel: 02 584 308 05   www.ristorantedonjuan.com
Open: 7.30pm–12.30am. Closed Sundays, first three weeks in
August and Christmas to Epiphany.   €55

Argentine restaurant Don Juan pays homage to its national dish, the steak – and carnivores everywhere. Here you'll find 100% Argentinian beef cooked and served up by Argentines in an authentic South American ranch-house setting. All manner of cow paraphernalia – cowhides, cowskin drums and horn hooks carrying cow lassoes – hang from buttercup-yellow and rust-coloured walls. Of the four dining rooms, the best table (and service) is in the grillroom, close to the action of the glass-fronted kitchen. Beef can be cooked in any of 25 different ways here, but its speciality is on the *parrilla*, or coal grill, which produces succulent, tender steaks the size of tree trunks, perfectly crisped on the outside. Be sure to save some space for their ambrosial *dulce de leche* desserts. A vegetarian minority is catered for, as are children, not least the (Italian) owner's son whose name was the inspiration behind calling the restaurant Don Juan. It's massively popular – there's a considerable Argentine ex-pat community in Milan, and the meat-heavy fare suits Milanese tastes. The spill-over is filling up its younger restaurant, Don Juanito (Corso di Porta Vigentina, 33; tel: 02 584 312 17).

Food 8, Service 7, Atmosphere 8

Eda, Via F Lippi, 7, Porta Venezia
Tel: 02 596 119 20   www.edamilano.com
Open: 12.45–3pm, 7–midnight daily. Closed second and
third week of August.   €50

Walking to one's table in Eda feels like the green mile down a Gucci catwalk, past a tiered audience of diners scrutinizing your ill-advised non-Gucci outfit. In fact the sharp, dark chocolate interior is so Gucci that the linaugurated its last designer's launch party here. Fashion friends Gianfranco and Marco opened Eda in March 2004 (Eda was in fact Marco's late aunt who said in a dream that the restaurant would succeed). And its simple formula is filling the till and the tables: traditional Sicilian cuisine (delivered in *nouvelle cuisine* style and size by beautiful and cool young waiting staff) in an aesthetically pleasing modern space, minimal but for eclectic touches such as tartan sofas and stuffed animals. *Aperitivo* can be sampled at the circular island bar, a live DJ takes to his decks at the weekend, and a classical quartet plays to brunchers on Sundays. In fact, it's surprisingly easy-going and friendly – although it does help if you're wearing Gucci.

Food 7, Service 8, Atmosphere 8

Finger's, Via S Gerolamo Emiliani, 2, Porta Romana
Tel: 02 541 226 75
Open: 8–midnight (1am Fri, Sat). Closed Mondays.   €70

It's chopsticks at dawn for the title of the best sushi restaurant in Milan but Fingers is right up there. Opened in summer 2004 by hip Japanese/Brazilian head chef Roberto Okabe, it has already hosted parties for Gucci, Calvin Klein and Armani. Its motto is 'creative'– there's not a drab slab of sashimi in sight. Roberto mixes it up with Italian influences; his signature dish is *carpaccio al gazpacho* – essentially sashimi with sauce and flavour. Forty different varieties of sushi are available, all loaded with lime, ginger, sesame, honey, etc. Desserts are bought in from Austrian maestro Ernest Knam and his Milan-based bakery Antica Arte del Dolce (the Milanese apparently haven't taken to

Japan's more lightweight offerings). For preferential treatment, sit at the sushi bar where Roberto's regulars are guinea pigs for new creations; otherwise there's the cocktail bar (where sake sours are sunk), a *tatami* area, lounge area, wicker chairs and tables, and summer seating outside. All is a sexy, softened take on

Japanese design with exotic flowers and candles: excellent taste all round.

Food 9, Service 8, Atmosphere 8

Giulio Pane e Ojo, Via L Moratori, 10, Porta Romana
Tel: 02 545 6189 www.giuliopaneojo.com
Open: 12.30–2pm, 7.30pm–midnight. Closed Sundays.   €40

Romans lament Milan's aloofness. In this modest *osteria romana*, it's easy to see the level of friendliness that they're used to. There is even a no-menu policy so as to encourage more conversation with the waiters. A tasty plate of *pecorino* and *prosciutto* awaits diners at their table, followed by *tipico* rustic Roman cuisine, such as *saltimbocca* and Giulio's celebrated pasta dishes that follow ancient peasant recipes. The restaurant is owned by Davide Ranucci from Lazio, Rome (Giulio is the name of his grandfather, whose farm still supplies the *pecorino*). There are three warm and cosy trattoria-style rooms (one is a new overspill out back to house an ever-burgeoning crowd). There are two sittings for dinner: 8pm and a less rushed round at 10.30pm, which is considerably more raucous. Group-friendly (although booking is essential) yet intimate enough for *innamorati*; hang around for long enough and you might start to think you chose the wrong city.

Food 8, Service 9, Atmosphere 9

Joia, Via P Castaldi, 18, Porta Venezia
Tel: 02 204 9244 www.joia.it
Open: midday–2.30, 7.30–11pm. Closed Saturday lunchtimes, Sundays and throughout August.   €65

Opening a gastronomic vegetarian restaurant in a city of carni-vores is a gutsy move. Yet Joia, under the charge of Swiss/Italian owner-chef Pietro Leemann, has survived as Milan's meat-free paragon since 1989, even spawning a satellite in Navigli called Joia Leggero (Corso di Porta Ticinese, 106; tel: 02 8940 4134). Leemann, who often roams the restaurant floor, has turned vege-tarian cuisine on its head, adding style and sophistication (and fish to some dishes). Witty, quirky food peppered with Pietro's Zen philosophizing brightens up an otherwise rather solemn atmosphere. Thus Egg Apparent is a faux egg of broccoli jelly with a joke yolk of pumpkin pesto. Presentation is key – Cubist in style – and painstaking. Prepare for a long innings: the slow service could be attributed to the chef's artistic licence; hurried diners should take the set menu or, better still, return with more time.

Food 9, Service 7, Atmosphere 6

Just Cavalli Café, Via L Camoens, Parco Sempione
Tel: 02 311 817 www.justcavallicafe.com
Open: 7pm–2am (kitchen 8–midnight) daily;
also 12.30–3.30pm Sun.   €85

Italian fashion designer Roberto Cavalli, famed for his flamboyant
furs and feathers, named the Just Cavalli Café after his diffusion
line. In true Cavalli spirit, this glass and brushed steel horseshoe
structure (situated by Parco Sempione's Eiffel-like Torre Branca)
is decorated with wild animal prints (from Roberto Cavalli Casa
no less), baroque crystal chandeliers, exotic flowers, mirrors and

a brace of Argentinian mastiffs that treat the place like their palace. And in true fashion spirit, the fabrics are changed seasonally. Be sure that yours are up to date, for this glamorous location is favoured by fashion execs, happy to pay over the odds for bijou-portioned modern Italian cuisine (style over substance, some argue). In the summer the surrounding garden and first-floor terrace, with muslin-draped Balinese beds, tropical plants and calico parasols, are opened up when the fashion flock come for *aperitivo* to graze on sushi, the accessory *du jour*.

Food 7, Service 8, Atmosphere 7

Lifegate Restaurant, Via Orti, 10, Porta Romana
Tel: 02 5411 6754 www.lifegaterestaurant.it
Open: 12.30–3pm, 8–11.30pm. Closed Monday lunchtimes
and Sundays.   €60

Being right-on in Milan is about as fashionable as a purple rinse. This is no obstacle to eco-entrepreneur Marco Roveda, who opened the all-organic, fair-trade, environmentally friendly Lifegate restaurant in 2003. Designed according to 21st-century trends (chic chunky black wooden tables and chairs, oversized statement lighting, whitewashed walls), this is eco-indulgence minus the hairshirts and nut roast austerity. Roveda also runs Lifegate radio (the restaurant's soundtrack) and *Lifegate* magazine (whose framed covers are used to decorate the restaurant). Lifegate's message is to reduce our impact: trees are planted

after every customer, much of the interior is reclaimed, and the food and wine – Mediterranean with ethnic influences – is 100% organic with many vegan choices. For transparency, the glass-fronted kitchen can be seen from the street – there's nothing to hide here. Opposite is Lifegate Café (Via della Commenda, 43; tel: 02 545 0765), a younger, more vibrant eatery with a pizza bar, bio-beer bar and all the same morals.

Food 8, Service 8, Atmosphere 7

Il Luogo di Aimo e Nadia, Via Montecuccoli, 6, Porta Magenta
Tel: 02 416 886   www.aimoenadia.com
Open: 12.30–2pm, 8–10pm. Closed Saturday lunch,
Sunday, and August.   €115

The single most important aspect of Aimo e Nadia is not, appar-ently, the Michelin-starred cooking (by Tuscan husband and wife Aimo and Nadia Moroni), not the location (a quiet western sub-urb), not the crowd (people wouldn't travel out here to see and be seen), but the raw ingredients. So important are they that Aimo and his grown-up daughter, Stefania, patrol the restaurant explaining the food's provenance: nothing is factory-farmed, much is wild-crafted, all is obsessively and seasonally selected from source. The innovative cooking process focuses on each revered ingredient to preserve its freshness, taste and texture – the very essence of Italian cooking. Certainly there is a serious,

contemplative air in this formal yet modern environment as diners savour the moment. Service, complete with food served beneath 'ta-daa' silver domes (that here suggest pride not pomp) and two sommeliers, is as you'd expect of a Michelin-starred restaurant.

Food 10, Service 9, Atmosphere 6

Milch, Via Petrella, 19, Porta Venezia
Tel: 02 294 058 70
Open: 8pm–midnight. Closed Mondays and throughout
August.   €60

Milch, opened by fashion friends Mauro and Christian, is very much the fashion establishment's establishment, with a recherché soundtrack to match. The clean kitsch décor of deep pink evidently caters for a fashion industry demographic: few heterosexual men would dine à deux here. Milch is so-called after an earlier incarnation as a *latteria* (dairy shop) – the original street sign above the entrance is a useful landmark in a badly lit street. The new motif, cartoon-like pink udders, is apparently the reasoning behind the magenta colour of the restaurant's walls. The owners say it helps you to feel better. They also ensure that all their main courses are low in fat, and always offer a cholesterol-free vegetarian choice. But it's not so ascetic – Milch's inspired modern cuisine always comes in big portions accompanied by side dishes, and they clearly have a weakness for chocolate, starting

with dining tables shaped like giant chocolate chunks and finishing with a full-fat chocolate-heavy dessert menu.

Food 8, Service 8, Atmosphere 9

Noy, Via Soresina, 4, Parco Sempione
Tel: 02 4811 0375 www.noyweb.com
Open: midday–2.30pm, 8–11pm; bar/café 8am–2am.
Closed Mondays and August   €60

Just off the high-street hell of Corso Vercelli, Noy (as in '*noi*', as in 'us') is a sea of calm in gentle waves of browns and creams. Built in 2004 on the site of an old garage, it inhabits a large industrial shell – even when full, there's still a restorative sense of space. Super chic and modern, it resembles a fashionable furniture showroom, and it almost is: all of the furniture is by luxury lifestyle store Habits Culti next door. Noy multi-tasks like the

best of modern Milan: breakfast starts with *brioches e caffè* to classical music on engulfing sofas; lunch is by speed-buffet on walnut chairs and tables; for tea, kick back in the lounge area with a therapeutic *tisana* (or herbal tea infusion); at *aperitivo* the pace is picked up by a live DJ; and for dinner settle in for a sophisticated Mediterranean spread in the restaurant. And of course, it's got Sunday brunch more than amply covered.

Food 8, Service 8, Atmosphere 7

Parco, Piazza Cavour, 7, Centro
Tel: 02 290 018 75   www.parcosushi.it
Open: 11am–12.30am Mon–Sat; 6.30pm–12.30am Sun.
Closed middle two weeks of August.   €55

In a city where sushi is ubiquitous, Parco is popular because it grasps the Japanese point of sushi: convenient, fast and civilized. Overlooking *Giardini Pubblici* (hence Parco) are two outlets side-by-side (there's a third in Corso Magenta, 14; tel: 02 720 035 20). Take the left-hand option (as you're facing them), or follow in the *carpaccio*-slim gym bunnies that often trot over from Milan's most famous gym, Downtown, to reward themselves with a nibble of *nigiri*. Park yourself at the black wood sushi bar for an upbeat scene, or settle into the inner sanctum with low lights and low-slung seating, for Parco's delicate flavours and delicate portions served on beechwood trays. Ironic 1950s Americana images of pin-up girls and Waikiki sunsets in kitsch gilt frames hang from cherry-coloured walls. By evening, the pace of the bpm is picked up and the sake sours begin to flow.

Food 7, Service 8, Atmosphere 8

Quattrocento, Via Campazzino, 14, Porta Romana
Tel: 02 895 177 71   www.4cento.com
Open: 7pm–2am. Closed Mondays.   €55

Almost off-radar geographically, Quattrocento's *raison d'etre* is to make its guests' trek worthwhile: its after-dinner parties sometimes go on till 6am, featuring big-name DJs and live music. Located on a dirt track 4km south of the Duomo and surrounded by a cheering sense of greenbelt space and its own garden, it is only accessible by taxi. Its four dining rooms, lounge and bar are housed in a restored convent from the 1400s (hence, loosely, the name '400'). The interior design is modern rustic with an easy-going ambience: slouchy leather sofas from Paris's *Marché aux Puces* and moss-green dining furniture are offset against exposed brick and chocolate walls. The creative contemporary Italian cuisine is a draw in itself: novel ingredients, good portions and good value. After dinner on Fridays and fortnightly on Saturdays, three live DJs play easy breakbeat, house and funk; one DJ is even stationed in the unisex bathroom. Nowhere here is off-limits to the party.

Food 8, Service 8, Atmosphere 9

Rangoli, Via Solferino, 36, Garibaldi
Tel: 02 290 053 33 www.rangoli.it
Open: midday–2.30pm, 7.30–11.30pm. Closed lunchtimes
in August.   €45

Rangoli is considered to be the best curry house in Milan –
telling praise since it bears the added scrutiny of being ethnic.

'Rangoli' is an Indian welcome sign: the restaurant is filled with *rangoli* colours and symbols like a typical Indian house, albeit with requisite Milanese refinement. A warm and indeed inviting environment awaits, traditionally decorated with Hindu statues, stencilled walls and carved wooden archways. Bhangra beats, Bollywood love songs and sandalwood incense create a mellow ambience that's best in the basement. Earnest Indian waiters in ochre saris bring *poppadoms* and *prosecco* on arrival, and eastern promise of pan-Indian regional cuisine from Rangoli's Indian chef. But don't expect any surprises – this is more like a beginners' class in Indian food (blame the market forces, since its bestsellers are *tikka masala* and *korma*). Presentation is thoughtful and stylish and vegetarians are well catered for, as are those needing a side of chillis.

Food 7, Service 7, Atmosphere 8

Sadler, Via Troilo, 14, Navigli
Tel: 02 581 044 51   www.sadler.it
Open: 8–10.30pm daily. Closed August and first week
of January.   €110

Just off Naviglio Pavesi is Claudio Sadler's small two-Michelin-starred restaurant. Having opened in 1995, Sadler has been charged with resting on his laurels. Not so – he is still producing award-winning food, but the blended beige design is rather last

decade; the fashion crowd recoil while the stiffs don't see any
problem: their majority makes for a rather dour atmosphere.
Sadler's secret is to keep things simple – no surprises, just satis-
fying, healthy food without too many tastes in one dish.
Traditional Italian dishes are lightened up, sometimes with a subtle Japanese influence and presentation (Sadler has another
restaurant in Tokyo), although the fanfare of delivering dishes
beneath a silver dome has not been resisted. The sommelier-
served wine comes from small Italian producers and international vintages. Highly recommended are Sadler's samplers: delicate
and sublime canapés and *petits fours*. Sadler enthusiasts can enrol
for an *alta cucina* masterclass at his cookery school, Q.B. (see
Play).

Food 9, Service 8, Atmosphere 6

A Santa Lucia, Via S Pietro all'Orto, 3, Centro
Tel: 02 760 231 55
Open: midday–3pm, 7pm–1am. Closed Mondays and last three
weeks of August.   €60

In a city that's all about who you know and who knows you,
Santa Lucia is an institution (albeit of Neapolitan origins). It
shamelessly flaunts its catalogue of celebrity diners with over
400 autographed portraits. There is even a restaurant camera
should a celebrity have left their supply of publicity shots behind.

Its walls serve as a slice of Milan's social history, documenting the changing nature of celebrity from silverscreen starlets to TV girls, glamour models and footballers (usually from Inter). Despite this, the menu is unchanged since 1928 and packed with Neapolitan pizza and pasta dishes, supplemented by Post-it dailies and dishes invented by demanding celebs and obliged by head chef of 35 years, Antonio, a Neapolitan colossus. *Battuta* – very thin steak with garlic, oil, oregano and chilli – was a request by Italian actor Toto and is now one of its signature dishes. Naturally, newsworthy types get preferential treatment with tables in the inner room while tourists are left streetside (be sure to specify when booking). Publicity-shy celebrities should steer clear.

Food 7, Service 8, Atmosphere 8

Shambala, Via Ripamonti, 337, Porta Romana
Tel: 02 552 0194 www.shambalamilano.it
Open: 8pm–1am. Closed Mondays and last three weeks of
August   €55

Something of a destination restaurant, Shambala is 5km south of the Duomo. Follow the trail of Milan's hip professionals in the latest SUVs for authentic Thai and Vietnamese cuisine. Owned by the same husband-and-wife team of Compagnia Generale, this is a grander version on a similar theme – ethnic food in a serene atmosphere with welcoming, non-uniformed waiters. Set inside a stylishly converted farmhouse, there are various dining zones for fine-tuning one's environment: big rooms, small rooms, a veran-dah, a *tatami* for crossed-leg seating, sake-stocked bar dining, amorous Balinese four-poster beds, and an oriental garden in the summer. Pilgrims to Shambala (which in Tibetan is a faraway mythical land of enlightened humanity) are rewarded with gener-ous portions of real Asian food that's not afraid of a chilli or two in a chill, yet glamorous setting.

Food 8, Service 9, Atmosphere, 8

Tano Passami l'Olio, Via Vigevano, 32A, Navigli
Tel: 02 839 4139 www.tanopassamilolio.it
Open: 8–11.30pm. Closed Sundays and August.   €85

The point of this restaurant is in its title, 'Tano, pass the oil' – it's a celebration of Italian extra virgin oil. If ever there were such a thing as an olive oil sommelier, owner Tano Geatano would be just that. For every dish (even the bread basket), Tano prescribes and administers the perfect oil. His self-taught knowledge is per-suasively technical, on regional varieties, pressing, density etc. With such attentive service, ably assisted by his wife Nadia, quali-ty reigns over quantity here with just eight tables seating 22 peo-ple. Charming, old-fashioned quirks such as the theatrical ringing of the doorbell by new arrivals, the unsynchronized chiming of various antique carriage clocks and a rattling serving trolley counter a rather restrained smart/casual crowd. Tano's accomplished chef Antonio produces creative Mediterranean cuisine with European influences while Tano takes care of an excellent European wine list and his own culinary speciality, sweet flambéed goat's cheese prepared at one's table on said trolley.

Food 9, Service 9, Atmosphere 7

Il Teatro, Four Seasons Hotel, Via Gesù, 8, Centro
Tel: 02 770 88   www.fourseasons.com
Open: 7.30–11pm. Closed Sundays and throughout August. €95

Ranked among Milan's top ten restaurants and housed within a five-star hotel, Il Teatro is for special-occasion dining. The main draw here is the food: the safe, modern décor, punctuated by business diners and paramours who are happy to trade ambience for privacy at generously spaced tables, makes for a rather staid atmosphere. Executive chef Sergio Mei, with two cookery books to his name, uses adventurous ingredients to reinterpret traditional Italian cuisine in four different menus – regional, seasonal, vegetarian and one for children. The comprehensive Italian-based wine list comes with extensive tasting notes and is served by a sommelier. If there is any theatre (a theme taken from the restaurant's name that is played up on the menus: 'Welcome to the show! Let the curtains rise!'), it's right there on the plates: this chef prefers to stay backstage. Book ahead for the best table in the house – the chequered banquette in the frescoed alcove.

Food 9, Service 8, Atmosphere 7

Trattoria Toscana, Corso di Porta Ticinese, 58, Navigli
Tel: 02 894 062 92 www.trattoriatoscana.net
Open: 6.30pm–2.30am (kitchen 7.30–1am). Closed Sundays.€40

Through a Narnia-like frosted-glass shop front on Ticinese's main drag is the family-run Trattoria Toscana set in an enchanted courtyard filled with trees, ferns and bamboo, and candlelit bistro tables and chairs encircling a central fountain. However, those in

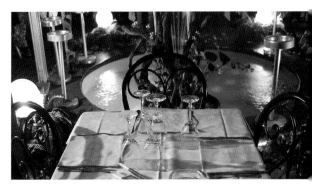

the mood for romancing should move on to the next review
– this is essentially a pre-club warm-up with big beats from the
large cocktail bar that charges the atmosphere with the right to
party. It's an institution of new Navigli, filled with a vibrant young
crowd all up for some action. The food and wine is simple and
tasty (and not Tuscan – that would take too long to make); with
only four staff in the open kitchen and a capacity of 170, expect
express classics such as *cotaletta*, pastas and risottos. It's always
upbeat, popular and packed, and great for groups; start early with
aperitivo. By winter, a forest of gas burners and roofing keep it
warm; in the summer the roof is raised – literally.

Food 7, Service 7, Atmosphere 9

Xe Mauri, Via Confalonieri, 5, Garibaldi
Tel: 02 608 560 28
Open: 12.30–2.30pm, 8.30–11.30pm. Closed Sundays and
throughout August.   €45

The name Xe Mauri (pronounced 'say' and meaning 'It's Mauri')
says it all – Mauri (or Maurizio, the Venetian proprietor) is the
selling point of this restaurant in bohemian Isola. Like a
Shakespearean court jester, the erstwhile set designer and artist
imparts his *joie de vivre* on every diner. Regulars say they make
new friends every visit, not least at the table of friendship – a
large communal dining table. This homely tavern on two floors,

with mismatched wooden tables and chairs, warm red walls, exposed beams and raw brick alcoves filled with kitsch is particularly conducive to a friendly, laid-back atmosphere. Venetian fish is always the speciality on the hand-painted menus (by Mauri's own talented hand), typically cooked *agro dolce* in vinegar and sugar, and mixed up with international influences (French or Spanish, for example). Heaven forbid should Mauri have to research any such influences personally and leave diners to it.

Food 8, Service 8, Atmosphere 9

drink . . .

There's a good reason why the Milanese are able to hold their drink better than their northern neighbours – it's thanks to the citywide ritual of *aperitivo*. At the cocktail hour (roughly between 6.30 and 10pm), virtually all bars lay out a *tapas*-like spread of *salami*, cheeses, crudités, olives, breads, which is free with the happy-hour priced drinks. Although one could easily forage for dinner here (as students are known to), it's extremely civilized and the Milanese are rarely greedy. *Aperitivo* institutions include Exploit, Roïalto and Da Claudio. Swankier establishments, including Dolce & Gabbana and Marino alla Scala, present salvers of *amuses-bouches* directly to your table.

More recent is the trend for Sunday (and now Saturday) brunch, where the Milanese eat through their weekend hangovers. Most offer Italo/American buffets of eggs, bacon, cereals, fruits, seafood, hot dishes, cheeses and cakes – it's very easy to over-indulge, not least at the Diana Garden, Alchimia and Le Biciclette – and they're always busy, so booking ahead at the top bars is advised.

A less favourable trend is that of the *cassa* system, akin to a Russian bread line, where you have to queue to buy tokens at the till first, then trade tokens for drinks at the bar – don't join a bar crush without checking their system.

The Milanese bar scene is very sophisticated – it's telling that it boasts the first international Ice Bar out of Sweden. And the cocktail craze has raised the bar: it's usual to receive an elaborate knickerbocker-glory-like creation, although often there's no menu: just tell the barman your favourite ingredients. The old classics are always popular and the noxious *negroni* (gin, Campari and sweet vermouth) is still a favourite – perhaps the quinine content wards off the summer plague of mosquitoes; or perhaps the high alcohol content numbs the irritation. Bar Basso's are the biggest and the best.

Taking their lead from the other fashion capitals, many bars multi-task as cafés and restaurants, catering for all needs from dawn till after dark and most offering table service; cafés and restaurants have also branched out with brunch and *aperitivo*. The action starts early and ends late: most bars are open until 2am and clubs till 5am and activity is concentrated around Corso Como and Navigli.

Social codes are quite powerful in Milan – worth mentioning since most bars cater for one or other social tribe (and you might have to dress to suit). The *borghese* (bourgeois) like a modern and glamorous lounge bar with lounge music – nothing too controversial. The fashion crowd likes things a bit more kooky – obscure art references and obscure music, as catered for at Trottoir, Cuore and Atomic. Actually, most bars exhibit art, but it's more commercial than art per se. Young local artists get to show (and sell) their art for free, and bar owners get free displays, and often a cut of the sale. Brand sponsorship is also massive in Milan – this is not Italy's commercial capital for nothing. 'Decorative' displays of Absolut, Heineken and Veuve Clicquot have paid to be there.

From May to September, Milan's bar scene spills outside and there are special outdoor venues only open in the summer (all, however, shut up shop in August). The best are Lounge Paradise at Piscina Solari, the first swimming-pool bar in Milan (Via Montevideo, 20; tel: 335 539 5082) and Bar Bianco, a cocktail bar in Parco Sempione with a live DJ (Viale Ibsen; tel: 02 864 511 76).

10 Corso Como Café, Corso Como, 10, Garibaldi
Tel: 02 290 135 81   www.10Corsocomo.com
Open: 11am–3.30pm, 7pm–midnight daily.
Closed third week of August.

The menu for the courtyard café at Milan's most important fashion boutique reveals much about the place. Most important, on page one, is the playlist from its own compilation CDs. Just one page of spartan food options (who's here to eat, anyway?) follows

pages and pages of cocktails, plus house rules (mobiles off – inevitably disobeyed) and details of implements used in the café (all available to buy). The experience is more like a lifestyle lesson according to the scriptures of Carla Sozzani, Italy's high priestess of fashion and curator/owner of 10 Corso Como. Of course, she does have exquisite taste – this is a magical garden café, with circular-themed garden furniture (it's all those o's in 10 Corso Como) among a colonnade of gas burners; by night it is illuminated by a canopy of starry fairy-lights. Service is fashionably late (lofty staff multi-task between here and the restaurant); time is best passed observing the fashion circus feed its shopping habit.

Alchimia, Via Brioschi, 17, Navigli
Tel: 02 835 6412
Open: midday–2.30pm (4pm Sun) and 6.30pm–2am Closed
Saturday lunchtimes, Mondays and last three weeks of August.

Alchimia's warehouse lounge bar, filled with 20th-century antiques by Castiglioni, Artemide and B&B Italia, feels rather like a vintage furniture superstore. Actually, the idea – of photographer/antiques dealer Angelo and his two grown-up children

Cristian and Valentina – was to create a warm living-room ambience, but at 400m^2 (in Angelo's old photographic studio) and with a capacity of 700, that's a lot of living. It's a mixed-up, shook-up world with three individual tastes ranging from 17th-century marble Tuscan statues to the 1930s art-deco wooden bar shipped over from Chicago – and it's perfectly deliberate (and tasteful), hence the name Alchimia (alchemy). Thoughtfully, there are coat stands everywhere to avoid the formality of cloak-rooms, and a steak restaurant dominates a large corner, where Argentine and Italian beef cooked on volcanic rock is served. CDs like 'The Best Chill Out Album Ever' and 'Mega Euro Lounge' are less auspicious; live jazz on Thursdays is much more in keeping.

ATM Bar, Bastioni di Porta Volta, 15, Parco Sempione
Tel: 02 655 2365
Open: 11am–3pm, 6pm–2am. Closed Sundays and throughout August.

ATM is named after Milan's transport system, Azienda Trasporti Municipale, since it is housed in a former ATM bus shelter.

Positioned in the middle of a traffic island, this long, skinny glass-fronted building can feel rather like a night bus going nowhere after a few *negroni*. There are no markings outside, although ATM needs no introduction as it emits a welcoming orange halo. In the summer it is visible for the crowd – an unpretentious professional bunch – that overflows onto the large pavement to sit on their parked-up Vespas. Its love-worn, rather 1990s Spanish décor is a cheerful mix of caramel, copper and coloured mosaics, plus the usual Milan trademarks of chandeliers, gilt mirrors and baroque velvet couches. Tasty Mediterranean lunches, seven metres of bar food at happy hour, and a relaxed, warm buzz make this a perennial, if now lacklustre, favourite. A radical refurbishment to include a second storey is imminent – and under the same management as hip bars Fresco and Fresco Art, comes with promise equal to three buses arriving at once.

Atomic, Via F Casati, 24, Porta Venezia
Tel: 02 890 591 69 www.atomicbar.it
Open: 9pm–2am. Closed Sundays.

Atomic shares the same witty retro look – and architects – as Cuore (see Drink) and Rocket (see Party) ; however, Atomic has a darker side. With soft-porn pin-ups by Marvel Comics illustrator Manara and surreal Hans Bellmar-style punk Barbies in pickle jars, Atomic attracts an outré crowd epitomized by Robert Smith-styled boys with make-up. Don't be put off, though – it's

lightened up with plenty of normal folk (in orchestrated scruffi-
ness) and comic 1960s details, starting with the red neon space-
ship street sign. The bar's curved wooden counter originally
came from Hotel St Moritz; the TV in the corner reads 'STOP
WATCHING TV'. At the heart of this small T-shaped bar is a
crazy-paved bronze glitter DJ den with a sun-like spinning dis-
coball where the daily DJ plays recherché electro, pop and rock.
Once a month it hosts *Verde Notte*, or 'green night' where
absinthe is added to the fray, wisely rationed in a bar where out
there is in.

B4, Via Vannucci, 13, Porta Romana
Tel: 02 583 056 32
Open: 6pm–2am daily. Closed August.

On first appearances, B4 ('Before') seems like standard fare in
Milan's bar scene – a perfectly nice, modern bar with lots of
comfy lounge zones, exposed brick walls and chunky cubed
leather furniture. And with modest ambitions, too – it is apparently so-named because it's somewhere to go before dinner or
before clubs such as Maggazzini Generali and Plastic (see Party).
But there's something intangibly compelling about B4: maybe it's
the crowd, a laid-back, artsy lot of young professionals; maybe it's
the location, away from any particular zone, it's frequented by
locals; maybe it's just its lack of pretensions. A non-commercial,
non-chillout music policy helps – as does its fresh, young art

exhibitions, generous *aperitivo* and quality cocktails. The barmen describe B4's good vibe as *legante* – 'bonding' (best left in Italian, as always).

Bar Basso, Via Plinio, 39, Porta Venezia
Tel: 02 294 005 80   www.barbasso.com
Open: 9am–1.15am. Closed Tuesdays and last three weeks of August.

This characterful cocktail bar always elicits a fond response from the Milanese, having historically introduced American cocktails to this wine-drinking city back in 1967. Its speciality is the lethal Milanese *negroni*, served in 1.2 litre glasses that are the size of flower vases – thankfully diluted with a brick-sized block of ice.

Bar Basso famously invented the *negroni sbagliato* (or 'mistaken negroni') when a harassed barman mixed a *negroni* with *prosecco* instead of gin – while it doesn't quite knock you sideways like a *negroni*, it still packs a punch. The L-shaped bar has two separate styles: an authentic 1950s cocktail lounge on one side, all in dark wood and with bijou tea salon tables, and on the other, the Sound of Music lounge, with an original and pre-ironic 1970s alpine chalet interior, frilly net curtains and twee flower-pots. Bar Basso is legendary among designers and architects who flock here during La Fiera to hail its *negroni* glasses – these unwitting icons are now available to buy, complete with a brick-sized ice mould.

Bhangrabar, Corso Sempione, 1, Parco Sempione
Tel: 02 349 344 69 www.bhangrabarmilano.com
Open: 7am–3pm Mon–Fri; 6.30pm–2am Sat, Sun; 12–3pm
Sun brunch. Closed third week of August.

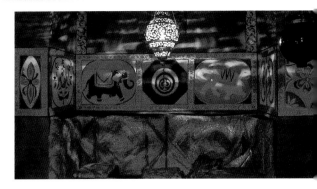

Bhangra beats are about the only Indian-themed feature that doesn't come as standard at Bhangrabar. With a Shiva room, a shoes-off people pile-up on embroidered sari scatter cushions, and a Ganesh room, an orange muslin draped space with a totemic Ganesh statue, every corner of this bar is covered with traditional Indian effects. The *aperitivo* spread is half-Indian with rice and (mild) curries. Barmen mix Indian rose, cardamom and *paan* liqueurs into fragrant cocktails (they also specialize in vitamin- and mineral-rich fruit and vegetable antidotes), while Kingfisher and Cobra are always available for the cautious. The bar is intoxicating with the sweet smell of Indian teak furniture, all intricately carved, some antique; the entrance door (from a grand Indian villa) and bar, previously in an Indian clothes workshop, are both over 100 years old. The DJ's pulpit, elevated to altar-like status in the main room, is beautifully ornate, making the garish euro-house all the more noticeable.

Le Biciclette, Via Torti angolo Corso Geneva, Navigli
Tel: 02 839 4177 www.lebiciclette.com
Open: 6pm–2am daily; 12–4pm Sunday brunch.

Inevitably, there's a story behind this name: built on the site of an old bicycle shop, Biciclette has capitalized on its history – with bike logos, glass floor tiles into the old basement workshop, and a mountain bike suspended from the ceiling. It follows the Milanese trend for sponsorship: owner Ugo, who also runs a

communications company, is marketing mad. Possibly with more sponsors than any other bar, Le Biciclette is almost like a quasi-trade fair, complete with plenty of freebies for its punters. Its hip and professional clientele seems to take this in its stride and the atmosphere is vibrant and relaxed. With the subtitle 'Restaurant and Art Bar', it serves contemporary Mediterranean food within monthly changing modern art expositions in a 1970s modern-retro restaurant. The bar area is both industrial and baroque, thanks to layers of diversely different refurbs since opening in 1998.

Cuore, Via G G Mora, 3, Navigli
Tel: 02 581 051 26   www.cuore.it
Open: 6pm–2am daily

Cuore is a plastic fantastic time-warp into kitsch 1960s Americana. *Star Trek* teleporters around the DJ decks play on the era's fascination with space travel; and a trailer-park tableau –

with vintage furniture around a TV set showing cult films such as *Psycho* and *The Sound of Music* – plays on 'apple pie' domesticity. *Hawaii Five-0* style cocktails – Pina Coladas, Mai Tais, Blue Hawaiians – come garnished with flowers from friendly barmen in Pan-Am crew shirts at the pink diner-style bar. Cuore's sense of humour is refreshingly offbeat by Milanese standards: even the name Cuore (heart) is apparently just a joke. Linked with Atomic (see Drink) and Rocket (see Party), there's a common, alternative outlook – and retro décor. Gay-friendly, free of lounge music, and even with vegan *aperitivo* on request, this is inclusive escapism into peace and love.

Da Claudio, Via Ponte Vetero, 16, Centro/Garibaldi
Tel: 02 805 6857   www.pescheriadaclaudio.it
Open: midday–2.30pm, 5–9pm. Closed Sundays and Mondays.

Less of an oyster bar, more a wine counter in a fish shop, Da
Claudio is probably Milan's most unique bar. Sadly Claudio, who
opened this fish delicatessen 50 years ago, died in the 1980s. His
successors astutely caught onto the trends for *aperitivo* and sushi
back in 2002 by serving fish *carpaccio* with *prosecco* – catching
two fish on one line, if you like. It's standing-room only – around
a central stainless-steel deli with banks of crushed ice piled high
with fresh salmon, scallops, oysters, langoustines etc. Point out
your catch to the salty seadog fishmongers in white coats and
wellies, who will serve it on seaside-holiday fish-shaped crockery.
It never stops being a fish shop and supplies lots of Milan's
restaurants and middle class, who choose their dinner over *aperitivo* to the tune of loud radio pop. It's unaffected and popular, in
a shipshape blue and steel setting with ornamental fishing paraphernalia all around.

Diana Garden, Sheraton Diana Majestic, Viale Piave 42, Porta Venezia
Tel: 02 205 81 www.sheraton.com/DianaMajestic
Open: 10am–1am Sun–Thurs; 10am–2am Fri, Sat.
Closed second and third week of August.

The Diana Garden – Milan's first hotel bar since 2000 – is an
institution, never more so than at summertime *aperitivo*, when up
to 800 people retreat into its beautiful private gardens for chichi
champagne cocktails. This fashion-savvy bar restyles its garden

every year with previous looks including Moroccan souk chic, 1960s Op Art and colonial South Africa. The interior, centred in a grand semi-circular Art Deco conservatory, is now doing the leather lounge look with pricey chocolate furniture by Italian brand Baxter. In fact, they're calling it the '>baxter lounge', like the Diana Garden is now the 'h club>Diana' (a veiled bow to its Heineken sponsorship). Despite this commercial sell-out, the Diana (its devotees still call it the 'Diana') remains a see-and-be-seen hangout. Its spectacular Sunday brunches are an exercise in

self-restraint: less of a buffet and more a banquet. Hugely popular (and expensive), there's overspill into the restaurant and 'Black Label Room', but peacocks book ahead for a table in the >baxter lounge – or Diana Bar.

DOC, Via Boccaccio, 4, Parco Sempione
Tel: 02 454 875 www.docmilano.it
Open 7.30am–midnight. Closed Sundays, second and third week of August, Christmas and Boxing Day.

There are dozens of excellent *enoteche* or wine bars that encourage a 'drink while you shop' attitude – i.e. a wine-bar-cum-off-licence. *Numero uno* deli Peck has the best (most expensive) wines and a sommelier-serviced cellar of over 5,000 labels, but, with a whiff of *hauteur* in the air, it's not the place to drain bottles of the stuff (see Shop; Via Spadari, 9, tel: 02 802 3161). Its polar opposite is Cantine Isola, a tiny, traditional and charming *'vineria con degustazione'* that's always brimming with locals (standing-room only), with poetry readings on Tuesdays (Via P Sarpi, 30; tel: 02 331 5249). Somewhere in the middle is DOC, a multifunctional gastronomy centre, with the clincher of a som-

melier on the shop floor to help when decision-making faculties have fogged over. Don't be put off by the Harvester-style décor – head straight for *la cantina*, the brick-vaulted wine cellar with 450 Italian labels all bearing the Italian quality seal *Denominazione Origine Controllata* (hence the name DOC) and cheery red-gingham seating.

Executive Lounge, Via di Tocqueville, 3, Garibaldi
Tel: 02 626 116 17
Open: 7pm–2am. Closed Mondays and the second and third week of August.

Walking down the long, softly lit pergola to the Executive Lounge is something of a symbolic drum roll. It's a fittingly cere-monious entrance to this vast Bali-inspired bar – a veritable vil-lage of cushion mountains and ornate teak lounge furniture topped by timbered beach hut roofs. Take your pick from low pouffes in shot-gold oranges, reds and pinks, sofas as big as king-size beds, and Balinese teak four-poster garden beds – the only thing there is no choice about is kicking back and getting horizontal. All the furniture and scene-setting Buddhas come from Bali, and the air is atmospheric with the smell of teak and scented candles and the sound of Eastern chill-out tunes. The Executive Lounge was opened in 2003 by eccentric Belgian socialite Maurice (who is usually accessorized with a ridiculously exotic cocktail – as standard from the bar), and the Executive connection is that the bar is situated in the garden of the ATAHotel Executive – the long walk to the hotel lavatories is sadly something of an anticlimax.

Exploit, Via Pioppette, 3, Navigli
Tel: 02 894 086 75 www.exploitmilano.com
Open: 12–4pm, 6pm–2am. Closed Mondays, from Christmas to Epiphany, and second and third week of August.

Exploit is a summer institution in Milan. Picturesquely positioned in the shadows of the ancient Colonne di San Lorenzo, here a democratic cross-section of Milan (i.e. everyone) spills out onto the large pavement terrace for cocktails at *aperitivo* time. In winter, the prime spot is in the brown and cream canopied veranda with burners and bamboo grasses. And with a subtitle of 'Drinks and Dinner', the requisite restaurant fills most of the brown and cream striped indoor space, with a Chesterfield-style padded tan leather bar at the back. Owned by the same duo as Living Bar, Fabio and Sebastian, its forte is in catering for a large crowd with quality cocktails and tasty *aperitivo* (and à la carte Sunday brunches). Its name comes from the previous bar here called 'Pois'; with a working title of the 'ex-pois', it became Exploit – pronounced like (petit) pois – when it opened in 1999.

Fresco Art, Viale Montenero, 23, Porta Romana
Tel: 02 541 246 75
Open: 7.30am–3pm, 4pm–2am. Closed Mondays and second and third week of August.

Like a lumberjack's lounge bar – all wooden planks and chunky industrial steel furniture – Fresco Art has applied the same winning formula as its sister bars ATM and Fresco: fast service, quality *aperitivo* and fresh fruit cocktails in stylish surroundings (conker-coloured leather sofas, moulded steel stools and teak

tables on wheels for easy rearranging). The cool crowd has taken the bait and comes here pre-Plastic (see Party). The 'Art' part does not, sadly, involve a modern Michelangelo masterpiece – it's actually no different from many bars here: a monthly changing exhibition by young artists who get to exhibit their work for free (it's also free decoration for the bars); but at least Fresco's alliance with the Instituto Italiano della Fotografia ensures a good standard. With its uninspired chill-out soundtrack, you might like to seek refuge on the pavement in the summer, when Fresco Art's capacity is doubled, not least by judges and lawyers from the nearby Palazzo di Giustizia.

Fresco Bar, Via Bramante, 9, Parco Sempione
Tel: 02 349 4576   www.frescobar.it
Open 8am–2am. Closed Mondays and third week of August.

'Fresco' apparently stands for freshness, fresh ingredients – something totally different. It was the first cocktail bar in Chinatown, opening in 1996 before it became an up-and-coming area. Refitted in Autumn 2004, this neon-lit white-cubed space softened with *fluoro* flowers certainly qualifies as 'fresh'. Its offerings aren't so different but it's hitting the spot for a sharp, creative crowd (run by the smart ATM and Fresco Art team; see above). More clinical than comfy, it's not the place you'd curl into a sofa (there are none) – with its minimalist (read 'hard') charcoal leather Zanotta chairs on bleached oak floorboards banked

by beech veneer walls, it's more the place for civilized fresh fruit cocktails. It prides itself on its creative Italian food – at breakfast, lunch and dinner, and à la carte brunches on Saturdays and Sundays, all from an open kitchen. Fresco's *aperitivo* focuses on quality not quantity – 'it's not supposed to be dinner', they say, refreshingly.

Frida Café, Via Pollaiuolo, 3, Garibaldi
Tel: 02 680 260 www.fridacafe.it
Open: 12.30–4pm, 6pm–2am. Closed lunchtimes Sat, Sun.

Frida Kahlo would be a fitting role model for Frida if indeed it were named after her. Notorious for being the first bar in Milan to sell absinthe (without limits) and for attracting lesbians for no other reason than its liberal outlook, Frida (for 'freedom', apparently) captures the essence of Isola's alternative ideology. And it does it genuinely – probably because it doesn't hide behind a glossy Milan-style veneer. Its fun 1970s psychedelia is not original but has been steadily put through its paces and 'aged' since opening in 2001. White-collar workers enjoy its daily-changing ethnic/Italian lunches, and all sorts assail it by night – pre-Pergola revellers (see Party), students, lefties, and regular folk who just want to cut loose. Music is anything from the *Top Cat* theme tune to 'Cool for Cats,' just no lounge music, because Frida says it is no fun – that is, according to the owners, a trio of ex-customers who liked the place so much they bought it.

G Lounge, Via Larga, 8, Centro
Tel: 02 805 3042 www.glounge.it
Open: 7am–3am (9pm Mon) daily. Closed second and third
week of August.

A mystery initial in a name is going to have any amateur sleuth
going. The management is evasive: 'It's G for Good Times, G for
Gucci, G like the G Bar in New York.' The penny drops – New
York's G Bar is for guppies (gay urban professionals). G Lounge is
the current style spot for Milan's in-crowd, and that includes,
although not exclusively, a snappily dressed gay fraternity (*en
masse* on Fridays). Opened in an old fascist club by the 'kings of
the night' Tocqueville/Divina consortium (see Party), it's a slick,
upscale venue on two floors. The small ground-floor bar is like
an acclimatization zone, with a fabulous fibre-optic chandelier
and a few token food offerings; the action is all in the basement.
Down a Bisazza-mosaic central staircase is an archetypal modern
Milanese lounge bar in a palette of white and chocolate, with
mock-croc furniture, jewel-coloured silk cushions and requisite
house music. A multitude of mirrors adds to the overall ambience of vanity.

Icebar, Piazza Gerusalemme, 12, Parco Sempione
Tel: 02 890 785 13 www.townhouse.it
Open: 6pm–midnight daily.

Being the coolest bar in town is easy when said bar has an ambient temperature of –5°C. An outpost of the Ice Hotel, Milan's Icebar is the first outside Sweden, franchised by boutique hotel Townhouse 12 (see Sleep). Everything in this glorified igloo – including the chandelier, furniture and glasses, and excluding the drinks, electrics, tourists and bar staff – is sculpted from 50 tons

of glassy arctic ice – from the River Torne in Sweden – which emits a glacial neon blue glow. Open since autumn 2004, the ice lasts for six months so the bar will be continually rebuilt and redesigned. Booking is advised – the entrance fee includes a 30-minute slot inside the Icebar, an Absolut Vodka cocktail, and obligatory silver furry ponchos and white wellies – not so cool. Afterwards a thaw-out upstairs at Townhouse 12's heated open-air bar, THerrace 12, where reindeer *aperitivo* and more Absolut is served, is highly recommended.

Living, Piazza Sempione, 2, Parco Sempione
Tel: 02 331 008 24 www.livingmilano.com
Open: 12–3pm (4pm Sun) and 6pm–2am. Closed Mondays and second and third week of August.

Living ticks a lot of boxes for Milan's *jeunesse dorée*: elegant surroundings, a black-clad like-minded crowd, lounge music, and a subtle sense of self-importance. And indeed Living offers many likeable elements, not least its modern, elephant grey and orange décor with plenty of parking options: barstools at the mother-o pearl mosaic bar, cosy corners heaped with matching patterned cushions, civilized leather chairs and tables; it also has a Mediterranean restaurant and over a hundred different vodkas. And with tall, arched windows that nod to the imposing neo-classical backdrop of Arco della Pace (Milan's answer to L'Arc de Triomphe built for Napoleon), you can choose your own entertainment: social observation or cultural assimilation. In summer, you can opt for birdsong over lounge music when the bar takes over the pedestrianized space outside by the arch.

Marino alla Scala, Piazza della Scala, 5, Centro
Tel: 02 806 882 95 www.marinoallascala.it
Open: 7.30am–10.30pm. Closed Sundays, August and from Christmas to New Year.

Another fashion designer's bar, Marino alla Scala showcases luxury leather label Trussardi – but it's so discreet about it, there's no actual mention of Trussardi. There are plenty of clues, however – it's right next to the boutique, on the ground floor of Trussardi HQ (with the Marino alla Scala restaurant on the first floor), the staff is uniformed in Trussardi chocolate shirts and trousers, and a large screen shows its latest catwalk footage. And of course, the bar's design – linear, modern yet classic – is right on-brand, with a clientele to suit: Milan's *beau monde* sits at the black volcanic stone island bar, framed by backlit frosted-glass columns. Execs (and Trussardi employees) stand at the corner coffee bar, while window-seated loafers watch the world go by in Piazza della Scala (its proximity makes this an excellent pre-Scala venue). Fashion swots might like to focus on the screen to watch and learn.

Martini Bar at Dolce & Gabbana Men's boutique, Corso Venezia, 15, Centro
Tel: 02 760 111 54
Open: 10am–10pm Mon–Sat. Closed from Christmas to New Year, and first three weeks of August.

Any Dolce & Gabbana devotee should make a pilgrimage to Dolce & Gabbana's Martini Bar – if for nothing else, to rest their shopper's shoulders since the bar is concealed within the men's

flagship store. It was opened in Spring 2003 by the design duo who were fed up with not having anywhere central and quiet to drink. In collaboration with Martini, the bar is a Dolce & Gabbana vision in trademark high-gloss black lacquer – a sexy circular space on two floors filled with Martini accoutrements; its modern chandelier centrepiece resembles a giant cluster of Martini glasses. Details are fittingly Dolce: black Dolce & Gabbana uniforms, Dolce & Gabbana Martini cocktails, even staff grooming by the Dolce & Gabbana *barbiere*. There's a rush of Saturday shoppers, but mostly it is as planned – quiet and exclusive. In fact it's rather like a living Martini advert during a lunch break; occasionally the stars themselves join the extras on set.

Milano, Via Procaccini, 37, Parco Sempione
Tel: 02 365 360 60
Open 6pm–2am. Closed Mondays and last three weeks of August.

Under the same ownership as the cocktail colossus Roïalto, Milano has applied the same formula to a (slightly smaller) industrial space. Countless pockets of retro leather sofas and armchairs are partitioned by bookshelves, bead curtains and foliage, and punctuated with 20th-century antiques and very low statement lighting. Collections of magazines and trinkets add a personal touch, while Indian bar staff all in white linen *djellabas* diligently craft fresh fruit cocktails – after you've paid for them at

the *cassa*. But even as a pared-down, less eclectic version of Roïalto, there's still so much detail that it feels like being in a lifestyle superstore. Located in Chinatown and frequented by the local ad execs, Milano has a glamorous, metropolitan vibe to it; its central marble and wood circular bar – the size of a round-about – comes from a Miami villa. All around is the calming sound of trickling water fountains – until someone trips on one of the many timber sleepers that support the 10-man sofas.

Nordest Caffè, Via Borsieri, 35, Garibaldi
Tel: 02 690 019 10 www.nordestcaffe.it
Open: 8am–1am Mon–Fri; 8.30am–9pm Sun. Closed Saturdays.

If you're craving a meaty political debate (hard in Milan when most are happy to go with the status quo), Nordest may be best able to deliver. Situated in leftfield Isola with a left-of-centre crowd, often to be found with their noses buried in *Il Manifesto* (Italy's Communist newspaper), there's a bespectacled, beatnik air to Nordest. This is apparently incidental, since its original objective back in 1996 was to become a quality jazz joint. Owners and brothers Cristian and Alessandro host live acoustic jazz every Wednesday and Thursday, and like their new neighbour Blue Note, expect the music to be taken seriously – no talking and no dancing thank you. Nordest is quiet and civilized, with classical music for breakfast and nostalgic rock'n'roll later on. Uniformed staff serve restaurant food and home-made cakes at varnished bistro tables and chairs (by summer, the bar migrates to the

hedged-in pavement benches). The thing to do here is enjoy unplugged jazz over a bottle of red or a grappa coffee and cabbies' manifestos at the bar.

Osteria del Pallone, Viale Gorizia, 30, Navigli
Tel: 02 581 056 41
Open: 11am–2am Tues–Sun; 6pm–2am Mon.

Italian football fanatics might already know that '*pallone*' means football. Owned by ex-national football player Mario Faraci, it screens all the big international and European league games. It's also a mini football hall of fame, not least for Mario himself, whose silverware and framed press cuttings are proudly displayed on the walls of this traditional tavern. National football memorabilia include sentimental artworks of historic games such as Italy's winning goal in the 1982 Spanish World Cup. Footballing heroes are said to hang out here, including AC Milan father and

son Cesare and Paolo Maldini, and with unusual impartiality, Inter players also throng here in equal measure. Service for its pub grub and British and Irish beers is likely to be *molto tranquillo* during the game, especially when Mario's team Juventus are playing.

Roïalto, Via Piero della Francesca, 55, Parco Sempione
Tel: 02 349 366 16
Open: 6pm–2am. Closed Mondays and last three weeks of August.

Housed in an old factory, the colossal Roïalto is something of a drinking factory itself. But with a sophisticated 1940s Cuban theme (and a 30-metre antique wooden bar shipped over from Cuba), it's classy and hugely popular. Choosing where to sit is the hardest task, in what feels like a wartime aeroplane hangar, teeming with niches of low-slung retro furniture in a jungle of tropical plants, Cuban antiques, modern art and kitsch. It's so big that there's room for this eclectic mix (there's also a restaurant, a summer terrace and a live DJ who plays imaginative tunes). And there's room for everyone – despite this up-and-coming street's remote location, all walks of life populate Roïalto. The only ('positive') discrimination seems to be with the choice of bar staff, all from the subcontinent of India (similarly at its sister bar Milano). Added to this leafy, forties cocktail scene it gives the bar a colonial feel. Join the queue at the pesky *cassa* system.

Le Trottoir, Piazza XXIV Maggio, 1, Navigli
Tel: 02 837 8166 www.letrottoir.it
Open: 11am–3am daily

Legendary bar Le Trottoir ('pavement' in French) captures the free spirit of old, crazy Navigli, with drag queens, Rastas, graffiti artists and radical anarchists all shaking the joint to live rock, jazz and hip-hop, and a piano for impromptu performances. Housed in a landmark *dazio* (an ex-customs toll gate on the Darsena docks), the irony of its location is not lost on this anti-establishment institution – which relocated from Brera in 2003 following a messy legal tussle with its landlord. One supporter, *noir* novelist Andrea G. Pinketts, was so outraged by the eviction that he chained himself to the building. His loyalty has been immortalized in Le Trottoir's Sala Andrea G. Pinketts, a fabulous psychedelic-yellow fairytale-frescoed room on the upper floor.

Apparently he does a lot of writing here, but concentrating among the combined energy of up to 600 revellers must be taxing. In fact, so animated is Le Trottoir that it sometimes literally rolls out onto the pavement – hence '*trottoir*'.

snack...

Milan's café culture broadly falls into three areas – anonymous salt-of-the-earth espresso bars, grand old *pasticcerie* (pastisseries), and a new breed of innovative cafés whose specialities range from chocolate to furniture. There is no room for Starbucks here – although interestingly it was the popularity of Milan's espresso bars that inspired Starbucks chairman Howard Schultz to launch his global chain. With the exception of the Princi – the Armani of bakeries and one of Milan's most successful, with five branches – Milan really doesn't go for chains. The vast majority are independent family-run operations, and most multi-task into serving alcohol, snacks and the Milanese ritual of *aperitivo* (free *tapas* at happy hour).

Most locals have a local café, which might seem like nothing special to an outsider but will inevitably serve excellent and cheap coffee and good chat. Similar to French *tabacs*, they're also useful for stocking up on sundry bits and bobs. None is listed here, but they are in their hundreds, all offering a window into real Milan.

The traditional *pasticcerie* are frequented by the ladies and gentlemen of Milanese society, and served by polite tuxedo-ed waiters. Men in cashmere coats and trilbies stand at the bar to quaff classic Italian liqueurs such as Fernet Branca, Ramazzotti and Campari, while matriarchs with meringue hairdos sit

down to froufrou cream cakes, silver cake stands of *pasticcini* (sweet pastry bites), *marrons glacés* and of course *panettone* (Milan's fabled Christmas cake – a light sponge mountain with raisins and candied fruit). Mostly these cafés cater for the Italian sweet tooth (for example, hot chocolates are thick molten chocolate), but occasional savoury offerings can be found hidden in stuffed croissants (*brioche farcita*) and most will oblige in conjuring up a *panino* on demand. Bizarrely, many also sell traditional wedding and christening gifts in lace and silver, and at Christmas and Easter time are ceremo-niously decorated respectively with *panettone* and *colomba* (similar to *panettone* but dove-shaped and sprinkled with almonds and minus the raisins). The best of breed are Taveggia, Cova and Gattullo.

Most hard-working Milanese don't usually indulge in long sittings but take their coffee and gossip standing at the bar, and always according to the coffee-drinking rules. The first is always the milkiest and then less so during the day – so cappuccinos first (with a *brioche*, the Italian croissant), then *macchiatos* and then *caffès* (espresso); in fact, *caffès* and *ristretti* (extra strong espressos) are acceptable at any hour. Drinking a cap-puccino after lunch would be as inappropriate as a gin before breakfast. Incredibly, there is little choice of blends in this coffee- loving city, and the Milanese are remarkably accepting of an Illy monopoly, perhaps distracted by flirty *baristi* who often craft love-hearts into their cappuccino froth.

Tea is becoming fashionable in Milan; boutique tea salon L'Arte di Offrire il Thé serves nothing but. Other speciality cafés, such as the chocolate paradise Chocolat, interiors showroom-cum-café Cantiere dei Sensi, and part-café, part design-museum Coffee Design, are all carving new niches in a market whose boundaries have all but blurred between bar, café, tearoom and bistro. Everywhere does everything here – coffee, snacks, home-made ice cream, cock-tails and even Sunday brunch. The only thing between you and gluttonous snacking is the ubiquitous *cassa* system (pay at the till first, order second).

Antica Cremeria San Carlo al Corso,
Corso V Emanuele II, 15, Centro
Tel: 02 760 217 67
Open: 6.30am–midnight daily.

Dangerously immersed in the tourist zone, this century-old café still hosts a very local ritual of *brioches* and *caffè* taken standing at the bar. Every *macchiato* and cappuccino comes decorated – at the least with a marbled leaf sculpted into the froth, and for *signorinas* with a flirty love-heart or even a winking smiley. Meringue mousse (soft and uncooked) is administered on teaspoons to stir into

espressos, or to take as a chaser. Specializing as a coffee bar, San Carlo offers just a few essential pastries and home-made ice cream, which in the summer can be taken at the pavement seating next to the pretty yellow San Carlo church. Its upstairs bar opens for the afternoon in a quaint, if worn, wicker-walled, oak-panelled tea salon, where *aperitivo* are served in rose-pink crystal glasses. To accommodate the tourists, San Carlo has opened an offshoot opposite (close enough to share the same address) but the Antica Cremeria still has the edge on history, charm and coffee.

L'Arte di Offrire il Thé, Via M Melloni, 35, Porta Venezia
Tel: 02 715 442   www.artedelricevere.com
Open: 10am–1pm, 3.30–7.30pm. Closed Sundays, August and between Christmas and Epiphany.

The Art of Offering Tea is taken very seriously in this dedicated tea boutique. In a delicate, tranquil, pistachio-green setting that's half-shop, half-tasting-room, the process of tea is presented. Brews of the world's best teas – from Kenya, Sri Lanka, China, Japan and India with some as precious as wild orchids – are perfectly measured, perfectly timed, and served at the perfect temperature. But don't go on an empty stomach – the tea purists frown upon breaking into the Earl Grey flavoured biscuits that are stacked up in Parisian dressers. It's just not the done thing to overload the palate. Of course all manner of tea trivia can be bought to take away, including teapots, strainers, Moroccan and Japanese tea sets, and even tea jam. There's also a *degustazione* on Wednesdays (booking advised), which is more like tea school and explains the ritual of tea. Just never utter the c-word (coffee).

Biffi, Corso Magenta, 87, Parco Sempione
Tel: 02 480 067 02
Open: 7.30am–8.30pm. Closed Mondays.

Biffi *pasticceria*, opened by Paolo Biffi in 1847 (who was famed for baking the world's then-largest *panettone* for the Pope), has changed little over the years. With polished walnut panels, antique Murano chandeliers hanging from high ceilings and scalloped white curtains, it's a classic traditional café with old-fashioned food and charming old-fashioned service. Fabulous ladies of a certain age, still styled in the 1950s, meet for cream

125

cakes at dainty tables while refined Milanese gentlemen discuss the day's business at the grand wooden bar over *caffè* and cocktails underneath an original Art Deco Biffi advert (the logo of which remains Biffi's mark today). A few additions – such as faux

Art Nouveau glass screens and new ownership – bring a sympathetic modernity to a civilized ambience, making Biffi an appropriate venue for post-*Last Supper* musings, or perhaps a sanctuary from Corso Vercelli's madding crowds.

Caffè della Pusterla, Via de Amicis, 24, Navigli
Tel: 02 894 021 46 www.caffepusterla.com
Open: 7am–2am Mon–Sat; 9am–2am Sun. Closed August.

A real cross-over café/bar, La Pusterla arbitrarily slots into Snack by default of its name. It's known equally for its outstanding

breakfasts, piled into the *piccola pasticceria* (really just an ornate glass cabinet) and served with 15 types of tea and all sorts of coffee, as it is as a place to drink good Tuscan wine after dinner. It's also famous for its wine cocktails, such as wine and sorbet floats and wine martinis. The kitchen is always open – munchies can be mitigated at any time with their *abbinamenti* – sharing plates of food matched to wine, for example, cheese and strong reds, *vin santo* and *cantucci*. It's always relaxed and always good value, there's plenty of seating spread over two old-fashioned tavern-style floors and it calls itself a *sala de lettura* (reading room) on account of its range of national and international newspapers delivered daily.

Cantiere dei Sensi, Via Carmagnola, 5, Garibaldi
Tel: 02 668 034 46   www.cantieredeisensi.it
Open: 7.30am–3.30pm Mon; 7.30am–11pm Tues–Fri; 8.30am–11pm Sat; 9.30am–5.30pm Sun. Closed second and third week of August.

Exemplary of Isola's gentrification is Cantiere dei Sensi (or 'site of the senses') – a café-cum-architect's practice opened in winter

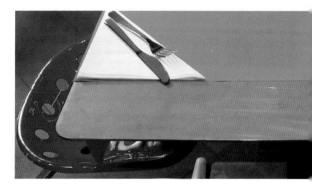

2004. It's ideal if you were thinking of employing this firm to redesign your house, since it offers a taster of just what you'd get – clean and contemporary urban interiors. The showroom doubles up as a highly competent café/bar, so breakfast, lunch

and dinner – and everything in between – is served among a functional display of product design: chairs by Philip Starck, Zanotta, Kartell etc., cutlery by Jasper Morrison, and as a tribute to the owner's late tutor and eminent architect, Achille Castiglione's lighting, stools and crockery. Everything is current season and everything can be bought – from the Bisazza mosaic bathrooms to the showers in the shop windows, or even a new-look house.

Chocolat, Via Boccaccio, 9, Parco Sempione
Tel: 02 481 005 97 www.chococult.it
Open: 7.30am–midnight Mon–Sat; 11am–midnight Sun.

As Milan's answer to Juliette Binoche in the film *Chocolat*, choco-holic Marina opened this tiny café because chocolate is her 'pas-sion' (her answer to Johnny Depp is apparently away right now).

Just as we drink coffee for energy, she believes we should eat chocolate for happiness; the petite Marina resists normal food so she can eat more chocolate. Her favourite is *fondente*, the dark-est 100% cocoa, which is in ample supplies in the shop, along with all sorts of Italian and Sicilian chocolates. Her hot chocolate is thick like chocolate sauce, and comes served in beautiful ceramics decorated with full-to-bursting cartoon cows.
Happiness fixes are also available from an array of rich chocolate cakes and brownies. There's a big focus on fresh home-made ice

cream, from an inviting counter resembling mini snowdrifts variously flavoured with white chocolate, Kinder eggs, and the best-selling *fondente* with chilli. Even the décor is choco-themed, with chunky chocolate cube stools and walls that look like they've been painted in hot chocolate.

Coffee Design, La Triennale di Milano,
Viale Alemagna, 6, Parco Sempione
Tel: 02 875 441 www.coffeedesign.it
Open: 10am–8.30pm. Closed Mondays and August.

Housed within the grand Fascist-era Palazzo dell'Arte and modern design museum La Triennale, Coffee Design honours its her-

itage with a working exhibition of iconic 20th-century chairs. The café – a large minimalist cube of white, grey and glass – is a blank canvas for 54 different chairs by the likes of Charles and Ray Eames, Jasper Morrison, Gio Ponti and Michele De Lucchi (the architect of Coffee Design). Along one length of the café is a low white wall of modern *objets d'art*, guest-curated by eminent Italian and international creatives. Along the other are vast glass windows that look out onto Parco Sempione and La Triennale's new Fiat Café (Tel: 02 724 341). Everything under Coffee Design's custody is sublimely stylish – from the (excellent) modern Italian food on chic crockery, to cruet sets shaped like conical flasks and test tubes, to an *au courant* crowd of Lenin-bearded architect types, en masse at its superb Sunday brunches.

Newcomers to the scene might like to accessorize with *Vogue Casa* from the bookshop next door.

Cova, Via Montenapoleone, 8, Centro
Tel: 02 760 005 78   www.pasticceriacova.it
Open: 8am–8.30pm. Closed Sundays and August.

Milan's most celebrated *pasticceria*, Cova is also one of Milan's most historic and most central, rebuilt in the *quadrilatero d'oro* in 1950 after Antonio Cova's original 1817 outlet near La Scala was bombed in World War II. A veritable chocolate box of a café, Cova

is revered by ladies of leisure, Manolo-weary fashionistas and tourists alike. Join them for an old-fashioned English tea with smoked-salmon sandwiches and cold cuts in the twee tearooms. Nibble on delicate fresh fruit *pasticcini*, or plunge into *Sachertorte* and decadent cream cakes; caviar and champagne cocktails are also available, all at a cost and sadly without much of a smile. If all this chintz is not quite your cup of tea, then the sweets-to-go from the *confetteria* – pralines, sugared almonds, *marrons glacés* – and fairy-tale cakes replete with marzipan ribbons, crystallized flowers and sugar roses make excellent presents and fantasy window displays.

Emporio Armani Caffè, Via Manzoni 31, Centro
Tel: 02 623 126 80
Open: 7am–11pm daily

Of all of Milan's cafés, this is the one for 'seeing and be seen'. Of course, it's most effective if you're conspicuously laden with Armani shopping bags, and since the Armani Caffè is just on the corner of 'Armani-ville', it's not a far distance to totter. Inside, a sharp young crowd with lapdogs and sunglasses dose up on vitamin juices. There's also a good selection of hot drinks and coffees, snack food and main courses, but since there are few fashionable cafés so centrally located, seats can be hard to procure and service can be forgetful. There's always the first-floor restaurant (Armani's second after Nobu), but the café, a cream space with a cubic steel island bar, filled with requisite Armani Casa minimalist furniture and enlarged Armani campaign pictures, has the edge on atmosphere and people-watching.

Fioraio Bianchi Caffè, Via Montebello, 7, Garibaldi
Tel: 02 290 143 90
Open: 8am–midnight. Closed Sundays and three weeks in August.

'*Che bello!*' and '*Meraviglioso!*' are the usual reactions on entering this florist-cum-café. Opened in winter 2004 on the site of Fioraio Bianchi, the original flower shop remains with the café added, namely a 16th-century wooden bar and 18th-century tables from Paris. Selectively decorated with fresh flowers and dried grasses and posies on every table, and with scrubbed terracotta tiles, turn-of-the-century radiators and dressers full of crockery, there's a nostalgic parlour-like charm here. All the

131

music comes from Paris, dating from the 1940s through to present day; smooth French jazz is played in the afternoons and evenings. The Francophile owner Massimo – an erstwhile bored

lawyer – wanted customers to step out of Milan (although there's no street sign) and into tranquillity. So food-to-go is not an option; slow food is celebrated, as is coffee, wine and grappa. After all of which, guests might be sufficiently carried away with the romance to buy a bunch of flowers on their way out.

Gattullo, Piazzale di Porta Lodovica, 2, Porta Lodovica
Tel: 02 583 104 97 www.gatullo.it
Open: 7am–9pm daily. Closed three weeks in August.

Unchanged since opening in 1961, Gattullo was the height of modernity at the time. Now it has segued into one of Milan's

finest traditional cafés – albeit with quirky 1960s frosted glass
chandeliers and retro sculpted wall-to-wall walnut panels. It is
still run by Domenico Gattullo and his wife and son – Domenico
is mostly in the on-site *laboratorio* harvesting the *panettone* (in
fact he now has his own 'pane-tummy'). The L-shaped café is half
bar, half tea salon: here just five small sugar-pink tables are lined
up along the length of a glass counter filled with hand-made
chocolates, *marrons glacés*, candied fruit and cream cakes. There's
no menu but most demands can be obliged, from prize-winning
panini to foïe gras and Iranian caviar. At the walnutty bar, its loyal
locals revere its *aperitivo* snacks and toast the bow-tied waiters
with the house cocktail of gin, vodka, Campari and Aperol, aptly
named the 'Domenichino'.

**Grand Café & Tre Marie, Viale Piave angolo Via Morelli,
Porta Venezia**
Tel: 02 798 800
Open: 7am–10pm daily. Closed second and third week of August.

The family-run Grand Café, open since 1953, certainly falls into
the traditional category – with a mouth-watering *pasticcini*
counter, grand crystal chandeliers, and a sweeping scarlet-
carpeted brass staircase that you might imagine Fred Astaire and
Ginger Rogers tap-dancing down (albeit in small steps). However,
with the input of the Montanaro family's grown-up children, the
Grand Café is unusually modern in outlook. A recent refurb, with

zebra-skin chairs, cream velvet banquettes and Irving Penn's black-and-white portraits of Dalì, Bardot and Hitchcock, capitalizes on the refined air here, amplified with jazz and classical music. English and Italian Tea Time menus (savoury and sweet respectively with fashionable Parisian tea by Les Contes de Thé) are served in the two tearooms. It's quite a departure from the Tre Marie chain (of which the Grand Café is a franchise), named after a charity that fed the poor. A painting of the original 15th-century *Three Marias* piously looks down on such indulgence.

Mediateca Caffetteria degli Atellani, Via Moscova, 28, Garibaldi
Tel: 02 365 359 59 www.atellani.it
Open: 8.30am–9.30pm (midnight in summer) Mon–Fri; 9.30am–7.30pm Sat, Sun.

Annexed to the Mediateca di Santa Teresa (a free internet library in a beautifully restored 17th-century church) is a large glass cube containing the Caffetteria e Libreria degli Atellani. With a

highbrow ambience, the café serves up the thinking man's crumpet in a serene, light-filled modern space that's conducive to profound thought. It also doubles up as a reading room for the specialist cinema bookshop, and somewhere to feed the brain after intellectualizing in the library. It is run by husband-and-wife team Piero (who has a classical TV channel) and Valentina (a historian), who will soon also be opening a *cinema d'autore* to screen art-house films. Even the café's name has blue-stocking associations, so-called after the owners' first bookshop in the noble Atellani family house (in Corso Magenta). The Mediateca is one of Milan's best-kept secrets – it's always tranquil, with affordable, contemporary cuisine and a summer garden; but then in Milan fashion always prevails over thought.

Peck, Via Spadari, 9, Centro
Tel: 02 802 3161   www.peck.it
Open: 9am (3pm Mon)–7.30pm. Closed Sundays.

On the first floor of Milan's best delicatessen is Peck Café. Whatever any of Milan's specialist cafés offer, Peck can probably also provide since it's housed within 1,300m^2 of gourmet food

and with its own 2,000m^2 on-site kitchen. Unfortunately there's no going off-menu but most tastes are catered for, with, for example, 125 seasonally selected flavours of tea (even noting a difference between 'breakfast' and 'brunch' tea), all served on Wedgwood bone china at wicker easy chairs and tables dressed with starched white tablecloths. There's a definite leaning towards the traditional, with Ritz-style Afternoon Teas (*Il Tè del Pomeriggio*), including tea, sandwich triangles, *marrons glacés* and *pasticcini* – just without the scones. Wine can be summoned from Peck's first-class wine cellar and is best taken with Peck's mixed plate of hams in the afternoon. Or there's caviar with cocktails – it's all the same at Peck's high prices.

Princi, Piazza XXV Aprile, 5, Garibaldi
Tel: 02 290 608 32 www.princi.it
Open: 24 hours daily

Known as the Armani of bread, ex-pastry chef Rocco Princi's
super-sleek flagship was designed by Armani's minimalist architect Claudio Silvestrin. His bakers wear Armani-designed uniforms and are visible to all though an internal glass wall that
flanks the *laboratorio* (kitchen) – park up on a red leather
barstool with a brioche and a *caffè* and observe them preparing
picture-perfect fruit tarts, pastries and breads. There is additional
seating outside on the bamboo-walled terrace by the Aprile
XXV marble arch. A vast variety caters for breakfast, lunch, tea,

aperitivo and dinner – from chunky olive bread sticks and hot
pasta dishes to *tiramisu* and *panettone* (listen for the bell signify-
ing fresh deliveries of warm bread). The bar serves coffee,
spumante, beers and cocktails; by night, Princi segues into an up-
market kebab shop as clubbers satisfy munchies on chunky slabs
of hot pizza. Princi has four other *panetterie* around town but
none is as chic or as busy as this.

San Carlo, Via M Bandello, 1, Parco Sempione
Tel: 02 481 2227
Open: 6.30am–9pm daily

Close to Da Vinci's *Last Supper* but tucked away down a side street, San Carlo (no connection to the San Carlo in town) is spared the passing tourist trade. A classic *pasticceria*, *gelateria* and *confetteria*, it's a bit thin on savouries, but is rich with olde-worlde charm and courtesy. Its literal 'tea salon' is prettily decorated with repeat patterns of quaint crimson teacups on vanilla fabric walls and curtains; even the tea service has this same teacup motif. Its banquettes of striped plum satin cushions are plumped after every sitting by waiters who are more like butlers, and Liberty details such as cornicing and stylized parquet flooring add to a sense of old-fashioned decorum. Fruit tarts piled high with fresh fruits, cakes in the shape of roses and ice-cream sundaes from its *gelateria* on Via Magenta are just a few of the indulgences on offer – there's no menu, but there's plenty of inspiration in its enticing displays.

Sant Ambroeus, Corso Matteotti, 7, Centro
Tel: 02 760 005 40
Open: 7.30am–8.30pm daily

While many of Milan's traditional *pasticcerie* still live somewhat in the past, none seems more of a time warp than Sant Ambroeus. With original 1930s décor as sugary as the cakes, majestic Murano chandeliers and silver rose vases on every peachy-coloured table, it's rather like a grand seaside tea salon, albeit a little dusty and weathered. This is an ideal spot to take a slice of cake along with an authentic slice of old Milanese society. Sant

Ambroeus's speciality is intricately decorated celebration cakes – from scale models of the Duomo to replica Caravaggio paintings, all made in the on-site *laboratorio*, along with the usual splendid fare of fruit tartlets, *marrons glacés*, candied fruit and so on. Canopied pavement seating serves Sant Ambroeus all year round, as do polite and attentive waiters, while the family owners like to think that Sant Ambroeus is served and protected by Milan's patron saint St Ambrose, hence the name.

Taveggia, Via Visconti di Modrone, 2, Porta Venezia
Tel: 02 760 212 57 www.taveggia.com
Open: 7.30am–8.30pm daily. Closed middle two weeks of August.

With an illustrious history dating back to 1840 that includes Austrian Empress Sissi hosting Christmas here, and more recently HRH Queen Elizabeth II buying its prize-winning *marrons glacés*, it's unsurprising that Taveggia is even the subject of some BA student's dissertation. All in grand Art Deco marble, tall ceilings and Rolls–Royce-like walnut panelling, it is quite unlike many of Milan's other traditional, more sugary cafés. Little has changed since coming to this address in 1907, although it is no longer run by the Taveggias but Lebanese brothers Roland and Simon. Bestsellers are still the *budini de riso* (rice-pudding pastry 'bombs') that historically lured Maria Callas to her regular table, and *panettone* as light as candy-floss; white tuxedo-ed waiters still serve old-fashioned cocktails in *coupes de champagnes* with sophisticated *aperitivo* of queen olives, parmesan hunks, *salami* and *tartini.* All that has been added is a bouncer on the door (Taveggia's stock is quite coveted) and a basement lounge bar called 909 (open till 2am), all bright and golden with mosaics, pillars and Versace furniture.

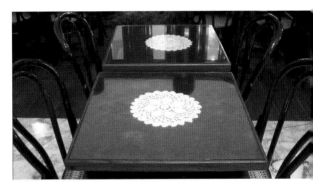

party...

While Milan's clubs are some of Europe's most glamorous – all crystal chandeliers and plush baroque furnishings – musically they lag behind. House music still
has the majority rule and the more commercial DJs emit apparently crowd-
pleasing sirens and cheesy rallying cries ('Put your hands in the air!' and the
like). Italian 'revival' music (i.e. radio pop from the 1960s to the 1990s) is also
very popular. Of course there are splinter scenes: as a backlash to all things chic
and glossy is a large hippie community that throws squat parties and raves
(Pergola is the best). The powerful gay fraternity has instituted an outrageous,
queeny scene – at Plastic and Gasoline – and Milan's rock music marginals go to
Alcatraz on Fridays and Saturdays (Via Valtellina, 25; tel: 02 690 163 52).

A guide to club talk is useful here: 'nightclub' means adult club; 'café' means
club; and the ubiquitous 'privé' is exclusively for VIPs. VIP status can often be
bought by investing in a bottle (especially with the more commercial clubs).
Costing €160-plus and to be split among a maximum of four to six people, this
will secure you a table and sometimes privé entry. Sometimes it's the only way
past Milan's rather *brutto* 'door selection' (in fact bouncers are so gruff that
they are called *gorilla* by the locals). It always pays to dress up. The vast majority
of clubs have a 'free entrance/obligatory drink' system where you have to buy a
drink to get an exit token (which amounts to an entrance fee). Keep it safe,
otherwise you'll be charged €€€.

The trend for multi-tasking has reached the club scene – many offer *aperitivo* and restaurant dining, although who needs one-stop convenience when it comes to partying? Some even do Sunday brunch (Old Fashion's in Parco Sempione is highly recommended). Many clubs offer live music and performance since it affords them generous tax breaks, and many are creative with closing time: a 4am closing can mean 4, 5 or 6am; the party generally kicks off after midnight.

There are set rules in Milan about which club when (important since it effects a queue/atmosphere trade-off). The Milanese are pack animals: on Sunday they all head to Plastic, to Old Fashion on Monday, Rocket on Tuesday, Hollywood on Wednesday, Gasoline on Thursday and Magazzini Generali on Friday. At the weekend, the Milanese drive to their country retreats leaving the Hinterland (i.e. the less sophisticated suburbanites) to infiltrate the city. For this reason, Saturdays are very commercial; Thursdays and Sundays are more interesting; Wednesday is often student night. Generally the most commercial clubs are around Corso Como and the more alternative are out on a limb.

And as with most businesses in Milan, clubs are generally independently run, but the scene is somewhat ruled by the 'Kings of the Night' – small consortiums that own several bars and clubs. Most notable are the rival owners of Divina/Shu/G-Lounge/Tocqueville and Hollywood/Loolapaloosa/Casablanca. Powers are then consigned to the club promoters who hold the key to your entry.

From June to September, the city migrates to its outdoor clubs. The best are Café Solaire (Idropark Fila (see Play); tel: 02 553 051 69) – located at Milan's artificial lake near Linate airport, and Karma (also open in winter). All clubs, like all Milan, shut up shop for some or all of August.

Armani Privé, Via Pisoni, 31, Centro
Tel: 02 623 126 55
Open: 11.30pm–3am. Closed Sundays, Mondays and throughout August.

Giorgio Armani's nightclub, in the basement of his Armani 'multi-plex', trumps most clubs in terms of style. Entirely fitted with Armani Casa in a neon-lit red, cream and black Japanese style, it's as if Nobu has been set in science fiction. Getting in can be troublesome, although reserving a table or saying that you'll buy a

bottle – in English – usually works (being international can be a passport in fashion venues). Bottles arrive on fabulous black lacquer trays: essentially mobile minibars with umpteen mixers and exotic fruits on ice. Commercial dancey pop soon draws you off your table to shake your money-maker alongside moneyed style slaves and smooth Tom-Ford-lookalikes. Be sure to do final checks in the hall of mirrors en route to the dance-floor because once you're there, smile – you're on camera. There's a huge screen (the sort that normally shows catwalk footage) that beams your own cringeful image on the dance-floor – everyone's a star in Armani Privé.

The Black, Via Canonica, 23, Parco Sempione
Tel: 02 336 039 07
Open: 11pm–4am Thurs–Sun. Closed July, August and first half of September.

The Black sounds like a rather undiplomatic aim at the black music market. And it's a good shot: once inside, this could be the Bronx – or Senegal, since it's bustin' with Milan's superfly Senegalese community, blinging with big chains, shiny tracksuits, Snoop plaits and fat cigars. And of course there's music to suit – R&B, hip-hop, rap and nu-soul. Things start off nice and easy with R&B, and crescendo into shithop (commercial hip-hop) – it's more crowd-pleasing than cutting edge here. Run by Maurizio the Black (white guy) in an old cinema, its leopard-print walls are punched with industrial circular lights, resembling a giant game of Connect Four gone mad (despite being styled on Studio 54 – although certainly its leopard couches look like they've seen some action). Bizarrely, Sunday is gay night with house music.

Café Atlantique, Viale Umbria, 42, Porta Romana
Tel: 199 111 111 www.cafeatlantique.com
Open: 11.30pm–4am. Closed Mondays and throughout August.

Decked out with blue mosaic tiles and stainless steel, Café Atlantique seems like a luxury, albeit dry, swimming pool, with a DJ stationed in a jacuzzi-like tub on the edge of the dance-floor. After a few Blue Lagoons, the Lost City of Atlantis seems like a more fitting reference, with the cascading fibre-optic chandelier that's like a giant jellyfish, and a sea of up to 1,500 people all getting wrecked. And there are plenty of opportunities to lose yourself, in the deep blue velvet Blue Room (with a second DJ),

the white harem-like tent, a spacey silver zone and a summer
terrace – in all, four bars and two restaurants variously cor-
doned off into privés during the night. Accessing them is easy
enough if you throw the readies at it – book a table or buy a
bottle. Music is commercial (disco, hip-hop, electronic, house)
and accordingly the crowd is mainstream and middle-class; pond
life is weeded out at the door.

Café Dalì, Largo Schuster, 3, Centro
Tel: 02 869 972 77 www.nylonpop.com
Open: 11pm–4.00am Tues, Fri and Sat. Closed July and August.

Café Dalì is a mini-club with a big cult following. And with performances from porn star Cicciolina, obscure art rock bands and
'post-punk kabaret' acts, Dalì himself would be proud of its sur-
realist outlook. Café Dalì, however, is keen to play down the con-

nection, and is tussling with its landlord to remove all trace of
him in the club – its fashion stylist management says it's tacky.
Sartorial standards are high here – 'nerds' are turned away, exhi-
bitionists and drama queens are in. Café Dali's crowd – stylists,
art students, photographers – have all but plundered Milan's vintage supplies. That's the scene here: glam rock, New Romantics,
go-go girls etc. Saturdays feature hostesses – an outrageous trio
of Betty bonkers who jolly the crowds in ever-changing outfits to
a soundtrack of alternative pop and 'queer rock'. Fridays are
much more street, with graffiti artists and skaters shaking it in
the hip-hop/drum'n'bass/reggae fly.

Divina, Via Molino delle Armi angolo Via della Chiusa, Navigli

Tel: 02 584 318 23 www.divina.biz
Open: 12.30–4am Thurs–Sat. Closed beginning of May to end of
August.

Divina is heaven for Milan's *borghese*. Underneath 'fashion' bar
Shu (now on the downturn of the cool cycle) and under the
same ownership, Divina is a chic monochrome space aglow with
UV and neon drinks trays that say 'look at me'. More than half of
the cream ostrich leather seating is privé, but then most of the
crowd – owing to its heavy door selection – are *fighetti*, offspring
of Milan's old money. Avoid being treated as one of the *popolare*
by buying a bottle, which comes with its own table and is delivered on said neon tray. Standing at the bar has some surprises –

stare into the middle distance at the lower bar and you'll find yourself right in the 'middle' of a nude mosaic; and the *cubista* (or dancer) on the upper bar will have you not knowing where to look. Music is accessible: ripped-up dance versions of cheesy pop – very Italian and very safe; dancing under the vast suspended flying saucer with flashing spotlights and jets of smoke is more hazardous.

Gasoline, Via Bonnet, 11/A, Garibaldi
Tel: 339 774 5797 www.discogasoline.it
Open: 11pm–4am Thurs-Sat; 7–11.30pm Sun. Closed mid-June to beginning of September.

As the black sheep of 'Corso Commercial' (that is, Corso Como), Gasoline attracts the gay gang, the fashion set and art students. Footballers and TV girls steer clear, no doubt freaked out by the psychedelic fluoro-pop designs, him-girls and her-boys and bizarre performance art from 1am. All in black and UV-lit neon, and a ceiling filled with quaking speakers, Gasoline is a hard-edged place that plays progressive trance, techno and hard

house – loudly. Thursdays are more easy-going, with Brit-rock, electroclash and revival music; Sundays are Gasoline's famous Gay Tea Dance – essentially a cruising club with go-go boys and drag queens. Door selection is very particular – first-time refusals have previously gained entry by stripping down to their

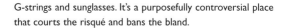

G-strings and sunglasses. It's a purposefully controversial place that courts the risqué and bans the bland.

Il Gattopardo Café, Via P della Francesca, 47, Parco Sempione
Tel: 02 345 376 99 www.ilgattopardocafe.com
Open: 6pm–2am Sun, Tues, Wed; 6pm–4am Thurs–Sat. Closed Mondays and throughout July and August.

In a deconsecrated 19th-century church based on New York's Avalon club, Il Gattopardo is similarly a temple to the boogie. But a brief sermon in Italian literature will illustrate where the likeness stops: Il Gattopardo was named after di Lampedusa's novel on Sicilian aristocracy – much more the reference here. The church structure is decorated like a sumptuous Sicilian

palazzo, with a neo-classical crystal chandelier the size of a small house, and ornate cream *chaises longues*. In fact the whole club is pure cream, like its sister restaurant and neighbour Chatulle (see Eat). Early *aperitivo* gives way to commercial pop and revival into the night, but at all times the guest list is taken as seriously as a holy writ: the management is keen to maintain the aristocratic theme. The only way in is with an advance booking – with this, Gattopardo claims to be the only club that is entirely privé. Call for your right to be a VIP.

Hollywood, Corso Como, 15, Garibaldi
Tel: 02 655 5318 www.discotecahollywood.com
Open: 11pm–4am. Closed Mondays, and from mid-July to end
of August.

The long-serving Hollywood is Corso Como's kingpin – famous
for being frequented by famous people, famous as one of the last
clubs to close (unofficially 6am), and famous for the gaggles of
international models that come on a nightly basis (where they
can dance off their excess 'energy' till the very end). Everyone
benefits: models receive free passes and VIP treatment, civilians
get to see a beauty pageant, and the stars get exposure on
Hollywood's Hall of Fame – brass plaques that line the entrance.
A king of reinvention since opening in 1986, it refurbishes every
year, always somewhat eccentrically: here, pagan gods and gold

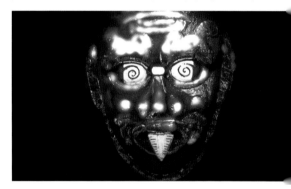

snakes. Musically it follows the trends of London and Berlin with
rock, house and rap (although still pretty commercial); 'Pervert
Night' on Wednesdays is a little more risqué with transsexual go-
go dancers. Its best feature is the two-way mirror between the
boys' and girls' lavatories, where narcissistic Italian men oblivious-
ly preen and pose. Hollywood also owns the less remarkable club
Casablanca Café opposite (Corso Como, 14; tel: 02 626 901 86).

**Karma/Borgo del Tempo Perso, Via F Massimo, 36,
Porta Romana**
Tel: 02 569 4755 www.borgodeltempoperso.net
Open: 9.30pm–4am Fri–Sun (also Thurs in summer). Closed last
three weeks of August.

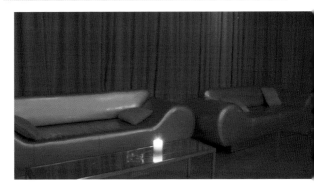

With a capacity of 10,000, this qualifies as a proper superclub. In
fact, it's two clubs – Karma and Borgo – side-by-side at the end
of a dust track way south in Milan. Karma is a privé club (accessible by table and restaurant reservations), while Borgo is for the
people. Arriving is like boarding an aeroplane: VIPs turn left for
Karma, cattle class turn right. But actually each is sufficiently
decadent, both with vast open terraces, making this one (or two)
of the biggest summer clubs in Milan – and still popular in the
winter. Karma's outdoor space is oriental-inspired with a plush
red baroque interior, and even a super-privé (Karma Diamond);
Borgo is like a traditional Sardinian village outside, with an eclectic and extravagant interior; music is commercial house, hip-hop
and disco throughout. Karma guests can access all areas – something of a poisoned chalice since there's a lot of scope for getting *perso* (appropriately, 'Borgo del Tempo Perso' translates as
'Place of Lost Time').

Loolapaloosa, Corso Como, 15, Garibaldi
Tel: 02 655 5693
Open: 8am–4am daily

After midnight, every horizontal surface of Loolapaloosa is covered with frenzied revellers dancing on the tables, chairs and even the bar itself. The bar staff only encourage such behaviour, by playing music that you can sing and dance to – pure chart pop

from the 1950s to now – and famously keep the bar's pendulum lights swinging in perpetual motion. And Loolapaloosa is famous on the strip, more as a disco-bar than a club for drunken folk who've failed the door selection at the bigger clubs. In that respect, it's an excellent, fun fallback plan. This ex-Irish pub is now owned by the Hollywood/Casablanca power-consortium, who has left its turn-of-the-century pub feel, wine-coloured walls and dark wooden furniture untouched. Needless to say, it has retained its Irish drinking heritage with a generous happy hour (5–10pm), and atmospheric memorabilia such as old Murphys and Guinness enamel adverts covering the walls.

Magazzini Generali, Via Pietrasanta, 14, Porta Romana
Tel: 02 552 113 13 www.magazzinigenerali.it
Open: 11pm– 4am Wed, Fri, Sat. Closed June to beginning of September.

For some, Magazzini Generali is the only club worth going to in Milan. With big-name DJs like the Chemical Brothers, and an out-there (for Milan) musical agenda of nu-house, electro, swing, breakbeat, and even DJ sets to live orchestras (Saturdays), it's a

serious club that's a lot of fun. Its Friday nights are the most popular in Milan, catering for 1,000 party-hardies in a two-floor warehouse on a desolate industrial estate. The house-heavy ground floor has two bars – its smaller, neon-pink bar on the stage is affectionately and unofficially called Gay Privé (because it's very gay and very fashionable). Livello 2 in the basement courts the hip-hop minority – it's a lot less serious down here. Emerging and established international bands play gigs here on non-club nights – it's not called the 'General Store' for nothing.

Nepentha, Piazza Diaz 1, Centro
Tel: 02 864 648 08
Open: 9pm–4am. Closed Sundays, Mondays and throughout August.

Nepentha is Milan's answer to Tramps or Annabel's: an exclusive old-money club. It is possible for those that don't qualify to get in, but take the wrong approach with the *brutti* bouncers and it can feel like purgatory (albeit surrounded by its habitués' Ferraris and Porsches). Instead you can phone ahead, offer to buy a bottle or latch onto a *fighetto* (those to the palazzo born). It's worth it for the spectacle inside. Cigars and champagne are on repeat order by men in blazers and shirts unbuttoned to new depths; women do the funky chicken in sequined cocktail dresses; all have Portofino perma-tans. It's a small club with a sea-blue and solid wood interior, rather like the dining deck of a gin

151

palace. The restaurant surrounds a small dance-floor, which fills quickly to cheesy old favourites. Service can be rude, but that's because they're just not particularly interested in new faces and new money.

Old Fashion Café, Via Alemagna, 6, Parco Sempione
Tel: 02 805 6231 www.oldfashion.it
Open: 9pm–4am Mon–Sat; 11am–5pm, 7pm–1am Sun.
Closed third week of August.

In a city that only does new fashion, Old Fashion might sound as appealing as 'out of fashion'. Indeed a veteran club (the oldest, apparently, built in 1933 in the Triennale's Palazzo dell'Arte), it's still going strong. Not least in the summer, when capacity grows

from 350 to 1,200 and spills into its 1,300m^2 garden inside Parco
Sempione. It's also big on Mondays as one of the few clubs open
in Milan – apparently when the other (off-duty) club owners and
dancers swoop down on Old Fashion for their kicks. With a
grandiose décor of red velvet *chaise longues*, gilt mirrors and
busts, and a lavish loosely North African theme, it still draws in
the industry in winter. This might be to do with the input of psy-
chology into the design – the many privé areas are positioned to
look down on the *popolare*: 'executive' tables and the restaurant
preside over the dance-floor and the privé dance-floor, is delib-
erately elevated.

Pergola Move, Via A della Pergola, 5, Garibaldi
Tel: 338 710 8159
Open: 12–4am Sat, Sun, and fortnightly Thurs. Closed mid-July
to beginning of September.

If you're looking for the underworld in middle-class Milan, give
up. But Pergola and the other *centri sociali* (Leoncavallo, tel: 02

670 5185 and La Stecca, Via Confalonieri 10) are as close as you
might get. Originally traveller squats (and still semi-legal), they all
offer raw hedonism (or squat parties) to all in the spirit of left-
wing solidarity. Pergola Move specializes in dancehall reggae and
drum'n'bass, and all that goes with that – Red Stripe beer, cakes
à la codename 'Maria Giovanna' and Milan's many trustafarians.

Don't expect anything salubrious – by day it's a dogs-on-strings haunt for political activists, with a hostel and vegan restaurant, and by night, the dreads congregate in what is at best like a basic student union with black and rasta-coloured walls. Prices are accordingly cheap, and the small entrance price is a 'contribution' not a ticket. But with a custom-built 10,000-watt sound system to big up the bass line, this is one serious reggae joint.

Plastic, Viale Umbria, 120, Porta Romana
Tel: 02 733 996 www.thisisplastic.com
Open: 11pm–4am Fri–Sun. Closed July to beginning of September.

Pop artist Keith Haring wrote in his diaries that Plastic was his favourite club in the world; Grace Jones and Andy Warhol have also been Plastic people. Since 1980, Plastic has always been on the edge: risqué, kitsch, and always very now. Its enduring success

lies in its ability to stay ahead of the game – by Milan's standards; it's one of the few places playing indie rock and French music (more breathy Brigitte Bardot, less MC Solar); also electro and 'sperimental'. With the proud claim of having started 'door selection' in Milan, offering to buy a bottle won't work here – it's just based on whether they like you (and your clothes). Glamorama is the word – drag queens, vintage clothes-horses and chic garçons all get the nod. Think camp and saucy to go with the décor: retro science-fiction, 1950s vinyl diner furniture, and a 'Bordello' room. It's most fashionable to turn up at 4, since it's open till 6am – unofficially, of course.

Rocket, Via Pezzotti, 52, Navigli
Tel: 02 895 035 09 www.therocket.it
Open: 10pm–2am Tue–Thurs, 10pm–3am Fri–Sun. Closed Mondays and throughout the summer.

Rocket breaks the mould of Milan's clubs – it's free entry with no obligatory drink, no exit pass, all in return for discorama and

big-name non-commercial DJs. Sometimes these 'big names' are big beyond music: Tuesday nights is 'I pretend to be a DJ', where decks are open to Rocket's favourite people, like fashion design-ers Alessandro Dell'Acqua and Antonio Berardi. This is *the* night to go to Rocket (and it's thronged with fashionistas) – but good times are to be had on any given night, to electroclash, under-ground 1980s and live bands. And with the same architects as Atomic and Cuore (see Drink), there's a similarly warm, retro vibe – here from the 1970s with lime flowery sofas, faux flocked wallpaper and brown vinyl stools. The idea was to avoid anything too contemporary and cold (and conventional) – and keep it relaxing and comfortable. People have become a little too relaxed in the past, even knocking a wall down by 'over-dancing' – just breaking the mould apparently.

Shocking, Bastioni di Porta Nuova, 10, Garibaldi
Tel: 02 657 5073
Open: 9.30pm–4.30am. Closed Mondays and from June to
beginning of September.

Less of a 'shocker' now, the name dates back to the 1960s when
Shocking first opened underneath Milan's Smeraldo theatre.
Custom-built into a theatre-sized space, it has been renovated

over the years, resulting in a mixed-up look of baroque gilt, oriental bamboo and steely industrial layers. But it's about the least
affected club in Corso Como – the poseurs go elsewhere and
leave the straight-up pleasure-seekers (peppered with a bit of
white trash) to it. Appropriately, VIP may as well stand for Very
Insignificant Person since anyone can get privé access by calling
ahead. Set on two floors, there's a large horseshoe-shaped
observation gallery from where said VIPs can look down at live
music performances hosted every night from 10.30 till midnight
(a cunning tax break), and prey on the sizeable dance-floor –
which after 1am is rocking with good energy, mainstream pop-y
house and crowd-motivating hollers and sirens from the DJ.

Soul to Soul, Via San Marco, 33, Garibaldi
Tel: 02 290 063 50   www.soultosoulclub.it
Open: 7pm–3am Sun; 9pm–3am Wed; 9pm–4am Thurs;
10.30pm–5.30am Fri, Sat. Closed from June to beginning of
September.

Soul to Soul is Milan's only other club that specializes in Afro-American music – but it's less ghetto fabulous and much more cosy, set in a 1930s gentlemen's social club. With a log fire, dark wooden panelling and original features like the solid wood and brass bar, brass pendulum lights and an apothecary chest, this is a curious yet charming little place. Of course they've 'bombed' the walls with graffiti – including a now-priceless piece by the late American graffiti artist Air One. And the brethren – from USA, Senegal and Eritrea – come to give 'nuff respect to Soul to Soul, although here the crowd is mostly white. The music – English, Italian and US rap, hip-hop and R&B – is easy-going yet conducive to working up a sweat. Live soul music with *aperitivo* is a gentle start to Sundays and Friday is the big night. It's all pretty relaxed, apart from the members-only door policy (but their tourist-friendly policy opens the door again).

Tocqueville 13, Via A de Tocqueville, 13, Garibaldi
Tel: 02 290 029 73   www.tocqueville13.it
Open: 11.30pm–4am; restaurant 9.30am–12.30am. Closed Mondays and from mid-July to end of August.

Right in the Bermuda Triangle of Corso Como's night spots, the Tocq sits in the middle of the club spectrum – not too hard, not too cheesy and pleasingly decked out in cubic lines with wenge wood, neon-lit Perspex columns and cream ostrich-skin sofas. The Tocq is one of many disco-restaurants, so clubbers must walk through the sleek, privé restaurant (with its own DJ) to the downstairs club that also has its own VIP area, bar and, strangely, padded leather ceilings – possibly for when the club blows off. And it does, to commercial house, R&B, hip-hop and Italian revival (different genres on different nights). Resident DJ Joe can often be found discreetly doing karaoke to Motown – done so

well that most don't notice. Understandable considering the volume of famous footballers and TV girls here – numbers are most concentrated on Sunday nights.

MUSIC CLUBS

Blue Note, Via P Borsieri, 37, Garibaldi
Tel: 02 690 168 88 www.bluenotemilano.com
Open: 7.30pm–1am Tues–Sun; midday–3pm Sunday brunch.
Closed Mondays and throughout August.

The Blue Note is undoubtedly Milan's most sophisticated jazz club – although its competitors are scant (see Nordest Caffè, Drink, and Scimmie, below). Modelled on New York's legendary Blue Note (since owner Paolo spent most nights of his 10 years in the Big Apple at the Blue Note), it shares the same cold blue design and love of the smoothest jazz. A high calibre of musicians, usually in black polo-necks, blazers and shades, delivers a mix of progressive and traditional jazz – hot, cool, acid, blues, soul etc. It's a very civilized (and detached) affair: a sensible crowd nods appreciatively, indulging in synchronized clapping if really impressed. Set on a large raised stage around extended restaurant seating, guests aren't obliged to eat from the Italian à la carte menu, but it's the done thing (brunchtime jazz is also available). Service is slow from young, inexperienced waiters – who possibly had an ulterior motive for taking the job.

Scimmie, Via A Sforza, 49, Navigli
Tel: 02 894 028 74   www.scimmie.it
Open: 7.30pm–3am daily

A genuine grass-roots jazz club right on the canal, this is where A&R types come to scout for new talent. Since 1981, Scimmie has played host to rising stars and establishment alike, from free jazz, bebop, New Orleans and soul to hip-hop and even British comedy. Having accumulated a few stories along the way, its walls and menus are proudly adorned with newspaper clippings and autographed publicity posters. A spontaneous crowd, free to dance and cut loose, has been known to jump into the canal in crazier moments – fitting since the name (pronounced 'shimmi-er', and meaning 'monkey') is from a Nietzsche quote that – "humans are more like monkeys than monkeys".

ADULT ENTERTAINMENT

Milan's adult venues are discreetly referred to as 'nightclubs', as is common in Europe; conventional nightclubs are just called 'clubs'. The Milanese like to think that this market caters largely for more primal foreigners – and in keeping, there's not much of a kerb-crawling scene; brothels are illegal. Its red light district is 'conveniently' centred around Piazza Affari, Milan's stock market (nearby to the Duomo). The best are the famous:

William's Club de Roi, Via Manzoni, 40 (02 799 252 www.williamsclubleroi.com). A plush red club in the *quadrilatero d'oro* that's been running for 50 years. **Top Town**, Via Baracchini, 7 (02 864 617 04). A well-known strip show with a privé. **Pussycat**, Via Gonzaga, 5 (02 869 2107).

culture...

While Milan is first and foremost a city of commerce and industry (it is said that it has more banks than churches), it still manages to tick plenty of cultural boxes: Roman ruins; colossal cathedral; monumental castle; world-class opera house, not to mention scores of theatres, museums and art galleries with price-less art treasures by Caravaggio, Botticelli, Michelangelo and honorary Milanese resident Leonardo da Vinci, whose *Last Supper* fresco is now protected by UNESCO.

Other famous inhabitants – including composer Giuseppe Verdi, architect Donato Bramante and romantic novelist Alessandro Manzoni – have all added to Milan's cultural heritage; in fact any given street in Milan is named after its virtuosos. Ducal families – first the Viscontis reigning from the 13th to the 15th centuries, followed by the Sforzas (15th and 16th centuries), have left their lega-cy, including Castello Sforzesco, a mighty fortress with its own 116-acre public gardens, Parco Sempione.

Because of its privileged geographical position, emperors throughout history have taken Milan as their seat. From AD 286 until 402, Milan (then called Mediolanum) was the capital of the Roman Empire – the best remaining relics are the 16 Corinthian columns (the 'Colonne di San Lorenzo') in Porta Ticinese. The Spanish Walls in Porta Romana are Milan's best-known reminder of nearly two centuries of Spanish rule (from 1535). In 1706, the Austrian Empire came for its share, building the neo-classical Palazzo Reale as their royal palace and commissioning various other institutions including La Scala and the Accademia di Brera (which now includes the Pinacoteca), all neoclassical in style with characteristic symmetry and proportion. In 1796 Napoleon came, saw and conquered, crowning himself King of Italy in the Duomo in 1805 (until 1815); grandiose neo-classical monuments, like the Arco della Pace and the Arena Civica, a mini-colosseum, were erected in his glory.

After the unification of Italy in 1861, Milan forged ahead as a financial and industrial centre, grand banks were constructed, much money was made and wealthy families built elegant houses (notably in West Milan around Parco Sempione); their deceased were commemorated in the new and prestigious Cimitero Monumentale. At the turn of the century, in artistic rebellion of mass production and straight lines, came the age of Liberty, Italy's take on the Art Nouveau movement (so-called after Liberty of London). The best of Liberty's curvaceous, organic designs can be found in the Cimitero Monumentale and its fabulous house-like tombs.

The Fascist party was founded in Milan in 1919, and commissioned gloriously pompous architecture (think Caesar meets Art Deco), such as the white marble Stazione Centrale (the city's main railway station, which is three times the size of the Duomo), the Palazzo di Giustizia and La Triennale. Milan suffered devastating destruction from air raids in World War II; rapid reconstruction modelled Milan into the modern industrial town that it is today, with the 1950s Pirelli tower as its flagship among a mass of less impressive concrete tower blocks.

For edited highlights, head straight for Piazza del Duomo for a climb up the Gothic cathedral and a browse through the 19th-century shopping arcade Galleria Vittorio Emanuele II. Top of the charts for entertainment is opera at La Scala, but getting tickets can be like trying to win a holiday to the moon. However, its splendid auditorium can be viewed via the museum. Most museums are closed on Mondays.

Basilica di Sant' Ambrogio, Piazza Sant' Ambrogio, 15, Navigli
Tel: 02 864 508 95
Open: 7am–midday, 2.30–7pm Mon-Sat; 7am–1pm, 3–8pm Sun.

The Duomo might have all the glory but Sant' Ambrogio is considered Milan's 'true' church. It was founded in AD 386 by the bishop Ambrose, who was canonized shortly after his death in 397 and is now Milan's patron saint. With multiple phases of construction over nearly two millennia, any trace of the church's

4th-century origins has all but gone, not least after World War II bombing and Napoleonic suppression, which saw its monastery converted into a military hospital in 1797. In beautiful red brick, it remains the most important example of Lombardy Romanesque architecture, originally built to commemorate two Christian martyrs, Gervasius and Protasius. Their rather ghoulish skeletons, dressed in white and gold ceremonial robes, now flank Saint Ambrose's in the 10th-century crypt. On 7 December is the Feast of Sant' Ambrogio, Milan's patron saint's day, which is centred on this basilica. It's the city's biggest festival and is marked with a spirited street fair in the piazza and flowing *vin brulè* (mulled wine).

Castello Sforzesco, Piazza Castello, Parco Sempione
Tel: 02 884 637 00 www.milanocastello.it
Open: 9.30am–5.30pm. Closed Mondays.

The Sforza family were lords of Milan during the Renaissance.
Their ducal residence, a colossal square-plan redbrick fortress
with great towers in each corner and a moat, was commissioned
by Francesco Sforza in the 1450s on the foundations of the 14th-
century Visconti Castle (Milan's previous power family). In 1905 it
was given back to the city of Milan after centuries of tumult,
including Spanish, Austrian and French rule; it now serves as one
of the city's most important museums (English guides available). In
the medieval castle's great halls, beneath beautiful frescoed ceilings and delicate stained-glass windows, are collections of art and
artefacts from Lombardian, Roman, Egyptian, ancient and prehis-
toric times; most notable is Michelangelo's unfinished sculpture,
the *Rondanini Pietà*. Idlers can just enjoy the views of this mighty
castle and its back garden Parco Sempione (previously the castle's
hunting ground, now Milan's answer to Central Park); at the west
end is Arco della Pace, a splendid neo-classical marble arch
designed by Luigi Cagnola in 1807 for Napoleon.

**Cimitero Monumentale, Piazzale Cimitero
Monumentale, Garibaldi**
Tel: 02 659 9938
Open: 8.30am–5.30pm. Closed Mondays.

More like the Elysian Fields than a humble graveyard, Cimitero Monumentale is the final resting-place for Milan's most illustrious inhabitants. It was built in 1866 on a vast 250,000m^2 estate filled with a dark, eerie forest of fir trees, and only supremely wealthy families and famous writers, artists and musicians are commemorated here. The imposing Romanesque Memorial Chapel in a large open courtyard reveals none of the melodrama in the ornamental gardens behind, where life-size copper statues of bereft damsels are dramatically draped over their loved ones' graves, while statues of angels keep guard over others. From the turn of the century, Milanese families appropriated permanent plots which led to grand-scale one-upmanship with ostentatious displays of wealth, religiousness and love. Elaborate mausoleums like mini-houses present a veritable timeline of Milan's social and architectural history, with an emphasis on Art Nouveau. The Campari family tomb is a replica relief of the *Last Supper*; the Branca drinks dynasty is also buried here, as are the novelist Manzoni, conductor Toscanini and poet Quasimodo.

Duomo, Piazza del Duomo, 16, Centro
Tel: 02 864 634 56 www.duomomilano.com
Open: 7am–7pm daily

This spiky Gothic megalith sits like a giant marble porcupine in the very heart of Milan in front of its own pedestrianized square. The world's third largest cathedral, covering 12,000m^2, it took more than four centuries to build, from 1386 to 1813, after a final push from Napoleon. Inside is cold, dark and majestically Catholic, with 164 stained-glass windows, 52 towering pillars and space for a congregation of 40,000 (there's always room for respectful tourists at Sunday masses). Take the 160-odd steps up to the roof (or better still, the lift; open 9am–5.45pm, 4.15pm in winter) for awe-inspiring panoramic views of the city (and the Alps on a clear day) through a gargantuan crown of 135 white marble spires. On top of its central spire, at 108m, sits *La Madonnina* ('little Madonna'), a gilt copper statue that is a point of reference for every Milanese. So important is *La Madonnina* that Mussolini

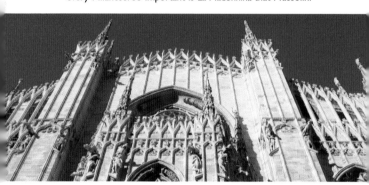

decreed that nothing in Milan should be taller. In the 1950s, Gìo Ponti's Pirelli Tower trumped her; to appease the city, the tower was topped with a scale model of her so she still had the highest vantage point in Milan (at 127m). The Duomo's history is documented in the Museo del Duomo (Piazza del Duomo, 14). Its epic construction has even acquired proverbial status: when something takes forever to finish, it's like '*la fabbrica del Duomo*'.

Galleria d'Arte Moderna and PAC, Via Palestro, 14–16, Porta Venezia
Tel: 02 760 028 19/090 85 www.pac-milano.org
Open: 9am–5.30pm. Closed Mondays and throughout August.

Milan's modern art gallery and contemporary art pavilion

(Padiglione d'Arte Contemporanea) sit side-by-side opposite the lush Giardini Pubblici, Milan's second largest park. The Galleria d'Arte Moderna is housed in the historic neo-classical *Villa Reale*, built in 1790 by Viennese architect Leopoldo Pollack (Napoleon once lived here; now it hosts smart wedding receptions). Spread over three floors and 35 rooms is 18th- to 20th-century art by European masters – from neo-classicism to Romanticism to

Impressionism and beyond, by Canova and Appiani; Manet, Cezanne, Renoir and Matisse; and Klee, Modigliani, Kandinsky, Braque and Picasso. GAM is currently undergoing restoration until the end of 2005 and only two rooms are open. Next door is PAC, a contemporary satellite originally built in the 1950s but bombed by Sicilian mafia in 1993 and completely rebuilt in 1998. An ugly mustard building from the outside and a clean white minimalist space inside, it exhibits starkly curated conceptual art. A small café upstairs serves refreshments intermittently.

Galleria Vittorio Emanuele II, Piazza del Duomo, Centro
Open: 24 hours daily

The Galleria Vittorio Emanuele II is a shopping arcade with Crystal Palace-like splendour: a 19th-century cross-shaped mall with four glass-covered halls that meet under a grand glass dome at a height of 47m. Fittingly for a fashion capital, it shares geographical status alongside the Duomo. But while it pays host to

the likes of Prada, Gucci and Louis Vuitton, blocks of fast-food outlets and hordes of pedestrian traffic are less alluring: fashionistas should head directly for *quadrilatero d'oro* It was built in 1867 by architect Giuseppe Mengoni and named after the king of the newly united Italy; it is affectionately called *il salotto di Milan* ('the drawing room of Milan'). Superstitious tourists can be found spinning around on the nether regions of the central bull mosaic for good luck. Insatiable tourists should cross the square to Palazzo Reale (Piazza Duomo, 12; tel: 02 860 165), the neoclassical royal palace built under the Archduke Ferdinand of Austria in the 1770s. Important international exhibitions, as well as the old imperial dwellings, can be seen here.

The Last Supper, Piazza Santa Maria delle Grazie, 2, Parco Sempione

Tel: 02 894 211 46 www.cenacolovinciano.org
Open: 8.15am–6.45pm. Closed Mondays.

Considering the difficulty involved in accessing Leonardo da Vinci's *Last Supper* – i.e. a two-week waiting list and a permanently engaged booking line – it's easy to feel defeated by a painting that everyone can picture anyway. But this fresco, completed in 1497, is all the more impressive having survived World War II bombing (after which it languished in open air) and having formed part of a stable during Napoleon's era. Now, tightly controlled conditions (two airlocks and a maximum of 25 people for

15 minutes each) only add to the drama. Despite 12 years of restoration and its UNESCO protected status, the fresco is still perilously faint, making it atmospherically ethereal. Depicting Jesus's announcement of betrayal, it was commissioned by the Sforza family to decorate the refectory of the Santa Maria delle Grazie convent. The adjoining Renaissance church, designed in part by Bramante, is also open to the public. Occasional standby tickets are available, but the committed should book online before departing (English guides available). Failing that, there are enough tributes and parodies around the city to get the picture.

Museo Poldi Pezzoli, Via Manzoni, 12, Centro
Tel: 02 796 334 www.museopoldipezzoli.it
Open: 10am–6pm. Closed Mondays.

Rather like New York's Frick Museum, Museo Poldi Pezzoli was originally the private palazzo of unmarried nobleman Gian Giacomo Poldi Pezzoli (1822–79), who bequeathed it to the city of Milan when he left no heirs. Born to art-collecting parents, Poldi Pezzoli augmented their collections on his European travels. Armour and weapons were his passion, and in the dark and dramatic neo-Gothic armoury, recently re-designed by Pomodoro, is a veritable iron army of 16th-century European suits of armour and ceremonial weapons. Room after room is devoted to his collections: tapestries and Persian carpets, Sèvres and Wedgwood ceramics, 16th- and 17th-century timepieces, books and lace and embroidery, including his own bedlinen. There's plenty of art as well, including masterpieces from Botticelli and Raphael. With its arched ceilings and elaborate cornices, the palazzo also gives a good idea of 19th-century noble life (English guides available).

Pinacoteca di Brera, Via Brera 28, Garibaldi
Tel: 02 894 211 46
Open: 8.30am–7.30pm. Closed Mondays.

Since the Brera Art Gallery is housed in the same 18th-century palazzo as Milan's Academy of Fine Arts, it's no surprise that it offers a crash course in Italian masters. The Pinacoteca is Milan's most important gallery, with over 500 paintings in nearly 40

rooms from the 14th to the 20th centuries, originally intended as the school's study materials. The content can be heavy-going, not least since many are religious works that were confiscated from Italian churches and convents by Napoleon. The collection now includes masterpieces by Titian, Rubens, Rembrandt and Reynolds, as well as Raphael, Mantegna, Caravaggio, Piero della Francesca and Procaccini. Slip off the audio-guide route (available in English) for modern works by Poliakoff, Braque and Modigliani, or go way back for Mycenaean, Etruscan and Roman artefacts. Botanists will appreciate the secret gardens; people-watchers will enjoy the theatrical portraits of Italian nobility in great dusted wigs and Brera's art students that drift around the grand court-yard (centred on a bronze of Napoleon by Canova).

La Triennale di Milano, Viale Alemagna, 6, Parco Sempione
Tel: 02 724 341 www.triennale.it
Open: 10.30am–8.30pm. Closed Mondays.

Built on the edges of Parco Sempione in 1933, the fascist-style Palazzo dell' Arte was designed by Giovanni Muzio to host the Triennial Exposition of Modern Decorative and Industrial Arts and Modern Architecture. While this three-yearly exhibition continues to run after 70 years, the palazzo is now a continuous foundation to all of the above, plus avant-garde fashion, photography and multi-media exhibitions (akin to Paris's Centre Pompidou) in 8,000m^2 on three floors. The Collezione Permanente celebrates Italian industrial design from 1945 to the

present day, with over 1,000 pieces from the likes of Achille Castiglione, Joe Colombo and Gio Ponti (Ponti fans should take the lift up his 108m high white-painted steel watchtower Torre Branca, built in 1933 for the Triennale for superb 360° views of Milan, just next door). Back in the Triennale is an excellent café (Coffee Design, see Snack) and art bookshop that specializes in rare publications on design and architecture.

OPERA

Teatro alla Scala, Piazza della Scala, Centro
Tel: 800 643 643   www.teatroallascala.org
Museum open: 9am–12.30pm and 1.30–5.30pm daily

To great traffic-stopping fanfare, La Scala opens each season on Milan's patron saint's day, 7 December. The streets are thronged with TV crews, police, well-wishers and often animal-rights activists (since La Scala's guests usually resemble a mink farm on the run). Built in 1778 for Empress Maria Theresa of Austria by the neo-classical architect Piermarini (who also designed the Palazzo Reale) and recently extensively restored, it remains superlatively sumptuous – all in red, gold and cream with an unfeasibly large chandelier (that takes 365 lamps) under a magnificently stuccoed dome. Six tiers of stalls with red velvet seats, jewelled curtains and gilt stucco run around the horseshoe

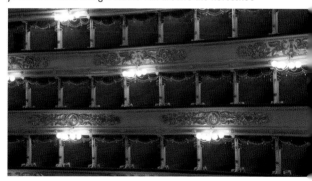

auditorium that holds 2,030 guests. It's usually fully booked up to two months in advance and black-market tickets trade for thousands (original cost around €160). The ticket office in the Galleria Vittorio Emanuele II sometimes has cancellations, hotel concierges might 'know a friend', and touts loiter in the piazza. Thwarted fans should visit its museum next door, which gives auditorium access between rehearsals (as well as exhibiting operatic paraphernalia).

CONCERTS

Auditorium di Milano, Largo Mahler, Navigli
Tel: 02 833 892 01 www.auditoriumdimilano.org
Open: 10am–7pm daily from September to May

While the Auditorium di Milano is trumped by the Conservatorio historically and architecturally, it holds its own with the latest acoustic technology and an accomplished resident choir and orchestra (La Orchestra Sinfonica). It was opened in 1999 in an old 1930s cinema, and the area surrounding it was widened to accommodate the traffic of musicians and audiences (and named after Austrian composer Gustav Mahler). Under the auspices of Musical Director Riccardo Chailly, it plays a traditional repertoire of Mozart, Beethoven, Haydn, Rachmaninov and so on, in a strikingly modern pearwood-panelled concert hall that seats 1,400 guests. Innovative fixtures, such as a children's programme, and a brunch-like Sunday sitting that serves up coffee and newspapers to classical music (11am every Sunday), attest to the Auditorium's modern status.

**Conservatorio di Musica 'Giuseppe Verdi',
Via Conservatorio, 12, Centro**
Tel: 02 762 110 www.consmilano.it
Open: 8am–8pm Mon–Fri.

Verdi himself never studied at the Conservatorio, North Italy's most important music academy – his application was rejected because they considered him too old. Evidently, the directors since realized their mistake and later honoured him by tagging his name to the title. The acoustically hi-tech main concert hall, Sala Verdi, hosts classical music concerts by visiting ensembles and Milan's Philharmonic Orchestra, which is composed of students and tutors of the academy. A smaller hall, the Sala Puccini, variously offers jazz ensembles, quartets and so on. Concerts are held daily; some are free, although advance booking is required. All – including a library with rare manuscripts by Donizetti, Bellini and Verdi, and an instrument museum – is contained within an impressive ex-monastery that was converted into this conservatory in 1803 after Napoleon's suppression of religious orders. It is attached to the dramatic church La Santa Maria della Passione.

THEATRE

There are more than 35 active theatres in Milan; all show in Italian, be it Shakespeare, Molière, Ibsen, Beckett or Brecht, although many plays are originally Italian, notably by 18th-century Venetian dramatist Carlo Goldoni. There's a good variety from the classical to the experimental, and the best are as follows.

Piccolo Teatro Grassi, Via Rovello, 2, Centro
Tel: 02 723 332 22 www.piccoloteatro.org

Influential theatre showing predominantly classical works by national companies, founded by producer Paolo Grassi and director Giorgio Strehler in 1947 in an effort to regenerate the post-war arts scene. It has an experimental arm at Teatro Studio (Via Rivoli, 6).

Teatro Litta, Corso Magenta, 24, Sempione
Tel: 02 864 545 45 www.teatrolitta.it

A grand 17th-century baroque palazzo with an 18th-century rococo façade, originally inhabited by the aristocratic Arese family, and followed by the Litta family; it underwent a massive renovation in 2003. Productions range from dance to classic theatre.

Teatro Manzoni, Via Manzoni, 42, Centro
Tel: 02 763 6901 www.teatromazoni.it

A grandiose classical theatre in red velvet and cream marble, the Manzoni is frequented by Milan's high society. Traditional drama is offset with *aperitivo* and modern music concerts by international performers.

Teatro Strehler, Largo Greppi, 1, Parco Sempione
Tel: 02 723 332 22 www.piccoloteatro.org

This modern redbrick landmark is an outpost of the Piccolo Teatro, named in honour of the late Strehler. It holds 1,000 people, and in the foyer has a mini theatre-in-a-theatre, the Scatola Magica ('Magic Box') for around 80 people.

CINEMA

Odeon Cinema, Via S Radegonda, 8, Centro
Tel: 02 869 503 22 www.medusacinema.it
Open: 2.30pm–midnight daily

The Odeon is to cinema what the Galleria Vittorio Emanuele II is to shopping – a formidable historical monument that has sold out to commercialism. Built in 1929 just off Piazza del Duomo, with three floors of cinema and a theatre below, it still retains much of the original Art Deco wooden marquetry, vast ceilings and marble floors, and following a recent conservation programme, some faithful reproductions of features such as cashiers' walnut and glass booths. But it's now just a façade for a mass-market multiplex. Screen 2 is the original theatre (still with period details), and original language films are shown daily in the small (and modern) Screen 6.

Spazio Oberdan, Piazza Oberdan, viale V Veneto, 2, Porta Venezia
Tel: 02 774 063 02   www.cinetecamilano.it

With a grand piano next to the screen to accompany old silent films, the *cineteca* at Spazio Oberdan is like a classic movie theatre, albeit in a sympathetic modern style (cherrywood slatting and charcoal leather seating). And despite Italy's nationwide preference for dubbing, all films screened here are in their original language with subtitles. The *cineteca* organizes its films into seasons – for example, on Charlie Chaplin and François Truffaut; there's often a retrospective slant, but this independent, publicly funded filmhouse is just as likely to present avant-garde video art. There's also a modern art space (La Galleria) and a specialist cinema book shop (La Libreria), and down the road, the Museo del Cinema (Palazzo Dugnani, Via D Manin 2B).

TICKETS AND TIMETABLES

Entertainment listings can be found in Wednesday's *Corriere della Sera* (the ViviMilano supplement), Thursday's *La Repubblica* (the Tutto Milano insert) or *City*, Milan's free daily newspaper issued at metro stations. All these publications are in Italian. Buying tickets from individual box offices can be frustrating: a much more sensible option for reserving seats for (pop or classical) concerts, theatre or sporting events is at a *biglietteria* (see below). Online tickets can be bought from www.ticketone.it (tel: 02 392 261), www.ticketweb.it (tel: 02 760 091 31) and www.ticketitalia.it.

shop...

Milan is something of a shopping Mecca, not least to the Milanese, who, *au courant* with this season's fashion agenda, never let standards slip. Even shopping trips themselves involve elaborate dressing up, and be warned: dressing down is often discriminated against. The wealthy majority head first to *quadrilatero d'oro*, Milan's 'golden rectangle' of fashion, a picturesque equivalent of four Bond Streets joined up in a square: Via della Spiga, Via Sant' Andrea, Via Montenapoleone and Via Manzoni. 'Gold' is appropriate since Milan's fashion is at its most expensive here, though since much is manufactured locally, prices are considerably lower than in New York, Paris or London.

Fashion's Square Mile is like the Las Vegas of fashion: dramatic flagships have lavish refits every year or so, adding VIP rooms, in-store ateliers and fanciful art installations. Many labels have three, four or five shops in the same few streets; all have a 'hands-off' air to them and white-gloved cleaners attending to offensive specks. Be sure to explore Via Borgonuovo and Via Gesù, home to Acqua d Parma and Brioni, while hidden in courtyards and piazzettas are more retail rewards. Don't expect anything too avant-garde: this prime real estate specializes in commercial Italian luxury. Most shops are open from Monday afternoon to Saturday evening, closing from 1 till 3pm for lunch; and the majority stay open every day in December.

Milan is also a centre for outlet shopping (although the Milanese are not interested in last season's fashion, leaving all the more bargains for less discriminating foreigners). The best is D Magazine, conveniently disguised as a *quadrilatero d'oro* boutique, while Corso Buenos Aires and its surrounding streets is Outlet Central. Out-of-town outlet malls offer whole days of bargain bliss.

Corso Buenos Aires and Corso Vercelli are Milan's answer to Oxford Street, with endless high-street chains and crowds to boot. The area surrounding *quadrilatero d'oro* from Via Dante to Corso Vittorio Emanuele II, via the beautiful, glass-topped 19th-century Galleria, offers commercial, low- to mid-range

brands. Of note is Rinascente, Milan's largest department store on eight floors next to the Duomo, where Giorgio Armani started his career as a window dresser. While it sells all the top names, it's touristy and unrefined. Ticking all boxes (fashion, beauty, interiors, toys, luggage, electronics and so on) and open from 10am to 10pm every day, it's useful for essentials.

But it's the lifestyle concept store that is having its moment in the sun right now. The much-imitated emporium 10 Corso Como is the best, although it knows it only too well, selling all one needs to lead a fashionable life, including clothes, accessories, interiors, books, gadgetry and CDs.

Via Brera and Corso di Porta Ticinese are welcome antidotes to Milan's purveyors of impeccable glamour. Brera specializes in young, offbeat yet elegant fashion amid an artsy setting, while Ticinese is the street scene of Milan with record shops and subcultures on the loose.

As well as fashion, furniture and food are also top priorities to the discerning Milanese. Italy's best names in cutting-edge product design and architecture are concentrated around Via Durini, while any foodie's first port of call should be Peck in Via Spadari.

10, Corso Como, Garibaldi

Named after its street address, Dieci Corso Como is Milan's most important fashion boutique, a concept lifestyle emporium of curated consumption from Milan's *grande dame* of fashion,

Carla Sozzani. Arranged around a pretty cobbled courtyard, the complex also includes a café (see Snack), restaurant, a three-room hotel (see Sleep), and Galleria Carla Sozzani, an exhibition space for eminent fashion photographers. On the fashion floor, every important designer is represented, with a lot of exclusives (including Azzedine Alaïa and Manolo Blahnik). It's quite an arro-gant affair: from the haughty shop assistants to the '10 Corso Como' logo-mania sewn into all clothes, this shop fully under-stands its own importance. Men's and women's fashion, acces-sories, interiors and beauty are on the ground floor, where shop-ping meets art in an ethno-urban setting. Trophy coffee-table books and CDs are on the first floor; po-faced shoppers from the smug, self-important Concorde set are all around.

Corso di Porta Ticinese, Navigli

A backlash to the recherché world of the *quadrilatero d'oro* is Ticinese's alternative street scene. Skaters, graffiti kids and even the odd punk and Goth hang out in the cobbled pedestrianized main drag (although be on guard for the trams that bulldoze through it). With Levis, Diesel, Gas, Energie and Carhartt, Ticinese is aka Denim Central. Picturesque like Portobello and individual like Camden, it's a nice place for a stroll, and there are plenty of places to park shopping bags and refuel: Ume for functional sushi, Coquetel on Via Vetere for fruity cocktails, Gelateria Le Colonne for home-made ice cream, and Trattoria Toscana (see Eat) and Exploit (see Drink) for drinks and dinner. Most shops are open on Sunday and closed on Monday mornings.

Adidas Originals Reinterpreted zip-up jackets and tracksuits, accessories and footwear from the trefoiled one's plundered archives

Antonioli Tiny but important boutique with select pieces from AF Vandevorst, Martin Margiela, Dries van Noten and DSquared, plus jeans and T-shirts

Armani Jeans Imposing presence in signature colours of red and blue with basement café

B-Fly Levi Jeans' boutique for limited editions, vintage and one-offs – the only one in Italy

Biffi Milan's original multi-brand boutique on Corso Genova, 6 – if it's sold here, it's made it to the mainstream: Luella, Yohji Yamamoto, Stella McCartney, Viktor & Rolf etc.

Carhartt Trademark baggy jeans, hoodies and the like from American skate brand

Diesel Concept store with denim gallery (including limited editions and superskinny jeans by Karl Lagerfeld), its high-fashion line Diesel Style Lab, and down the road, diffusion line 55DSL

Fornarina Young, colourful and quirky streetwear for girls

Frip Exemplary Ticinese store with in-store DJ, foreign fashion magazines and unusual fashion by new designers

Gas Affordable streetwear and denim for boys and girls from wannabe Diesel label

Marithé + François Girbaud French fashion house that's urban, edgy and sports-inspired

No Season Ticinese's answer to 10 Corso Como, with (mostly black) high fashion from Viktor & Rolf, Hussein Chalayan and Martin Margiela, and music, books and perfumes

Pane Cioccolato Hip chocolate heaven on Via De Amicis, 7

Purple Three stores: one with fashion imports like Fake and Swear; one with one-off pieces by artisan designers, and one devoted to hard-to-find (for Milan) trainers
Stüssy Cult surf and skate brand from California
Zeis Trainers and hoodies by Pony, Merrell and Pirello

Corso Venezia, Centro

On the periphery of the *quadrilatero d'oro*, some key fashion brands have chosen the strategic positioning of Corso Venezia to catch all the passing traffic of this busy yet scenic thoroughfare. All the important shops have lined the west side of the road that flanks the fashion square mile. Look above street level for rows of ornate aristocratic townhouses. Dolce & Gabbana's Martini Bar, concealed within its menswear flagship, is the place to stop for refreshments – and Martini (see Drink).

Borsalino Milan's most famous milliner: from top hats to suede crash helmets
D&G Dolce & Gabbana's younger line for men and women on two floors in a neo-classical setting
De Padova Coveted, colourful, contemporary furniture design and home accessories
Diesel Milan's flagship from cult Italian jeans brand; the toy-shop-like Kid store is just next door
Dolce & Gabbana Uomo One-stop menswear emporium, spa, bar and barbershop

Miu Miu Eternally fashionable menswear, womenswear and accessories from Milan-based Miuccia Prada
Vivienne Westwood twisted tailoring from the *grande dame* of British fashion

Peck, via Spadari, 9, Centro

A temple to 'Made in Italy' gastronomy, Peck is Milan's biggest and best delicatessen, spread over 1,300m^2 on three floors. A hunger-inducing array of gourmand savouries fills the ground floor: Parma hams, aromatic cheeses and Alban truffles, plus freshly baked bread and hot take-away dishes, both fresh from Peck's own 2,000m^2 in-store kitchen. The basement wine cellar

stocks over 60,000 (mostly Italian) bottles of wines, plus rare vintages, champagnes in magnums to Nebuchadnezzars and a sommelier-served tasting bar. Mouth-watering sweets, chocolates, ice creams and cakes fill the first floor, which also has a sandwich counter, tea salon and coffee bar. Opened in 1883 by Francesco Peck from Prague, it was bought by the Stoppani brothers in 1970; regular renovations have maintained this modern, light and spacious emporium as Milan's premier foodie destination; two Michelin stars awarded to its restaurant Cracco-Peck says it all (see Eat).

Via Brera/Solferino, Garibaldi

Running almost from La Scala in the Centro due north to Corso Como, these two streets are a welcome departure from the *quadrilatero d'oro*. The character here is much more individual, with unique boutiques selling younger, more affordable fashion. Wander off the main drag into Via Fiori Chiari, Via Madonnina and Via del Carmine for more offbeat fashion and furniture shops. National newspaper *Corriere della Sera* has had its offices in Via Solferino since founding in 1876, while Via Brera is home to the Accademia and Pinocateca di Brera (see Culture), so the area is defined by art students, art shops and small galleries, and the odd hack. Brera has become quite touristy so while there is plenty of choice for cafés and restaurants, prices can be inflated and street vendors await their prey. The Pottery Café is fun and cosy, the Centro Botanico is a healthfood shop with a tiny organic café, and Bar Jamaica is a riotous old institution.

AG Spalding & Bros Modern, metropolitan luggage, accessories and gifts

Anna Maria Consadori Eclectic boutique with modern *objets d'art* and furniture

Cavalli e Nastri Milan's best vintage shop with elegant finery from Dior, Balenciaga, YSL, Pucci and the like

Dilmos If Lenny Kravitz had a Milanese palazzo to furnish, he'd come here for 'functional art' – bold, modern and bizarre furniture

Germana Zama Elegant knitwear, interesting casualwear and

nice boots and shoes for men and women

Kristina Ti Pretty, young fashion that follows the trends of Italy's big players

L'Occitane All-natural cosmetics and toiletries from Provence

Miss Sixty Two floors of young, tight, attitude fashion from Italian jeans brand

Profumo Multi-brand beauty boutique stocking Acqua di Parma, Kiehls, Miller Harris, Creed and more

Shu Uemura Cult Japanese beauty specialists with a deluxe product range

Le Solferino Small but interesting shoe shop with elegant and mostly affordable boots, courts and eveningwear

La Vetrina di Beryl, Barbara Beryl's cult boutique on Via Statuto with quirky, un-Milanese labels like Eley Kishimoto and Y3, plus safe bets such as Miu Miu and Marc Jacobs footwear

Via della Spiga, Centro

Of all the streets in the *quadrilatero d'oro*, it is Spiga that is the by-word for Milanese luxury, with a high concentration of fine jewellers and Swiss watch specialists, two Dolce stores and two Prada stores. It's supposedly pedestrianized but that doesn't seem to deter wayward motorists. It's a charming street, all windy, narrow and cobbled, but such is the value of the real estate here that it has few cafés – slip off onto Via Borgospesso for lunch at Da Bice (see Eat), or for Bloody Marys at Four Seasons' power lobby in Via Gesù (see Sleep).

Anna Molinari Sweet, feminine high fashion plus Blumarine, Molinari's diffusion line in an industrial space with artfully tangled electric wiring

Armandola Gastronomic delicatessen (Naomi has famously microwaved her own take-aways in the back kitchen)

Bulgari Haute joaillerie, watches and luxurious leather goods

Chopard Precious jewellery, watches, sunglasses and trinkets in a pretty tea salon setting

Dolce & Gabbana Two extravagant emporia in black glass, mirrored walls, gilt and crystal, with womenswear in one and accessories in the other

Franck Muller Super-smart super-pricey Swiss-made watches
Gio Moretti Milanese institution with more than 75 labels
including Chloé, Gaultier, Donna Karan and Lanvin, plus furnishings, books and CDs

Helmut Lang Minimal, avant-garde mens- and womenswear
with LED poetry that runs down the stairs like an electronic
waterfall
Nulifar Important interiors boutique – the first in Milan to
bridge ancient artefacts with modern *objets d'art*, deservedly
expensive
Prada Two of Prada's six Milan boutiques are here – one selling
delectable underwear, the other womenswear and accessories
Roberto Cavalli With a 7,000-litre seawater aquarium and in-
store café, Cavalli is the new titleholder of Milan's most showy
shop
Ruffo Men's and women's boutiques side-by-side from high-end
Italian leather house
Il Salumeria di Montenapoleone Great hocks of Parma ham,
Italian cheeses, olives and pastas, plus courtyard restaurant
Tiffany & Co Signature silverware, in a rather tired setting by
Spiga's standards
Tods Rubber-studded driving shoes and more from this Milan-
based luxury leather label

Via Durini, Centro

Just east of the *quadrilatero d'oro* is this specialist interiors street.

Milan is something of a specialist interiors city, with its world-famous furniture fair La Fiera, every April, and a population of architects comparable to miners in Newcastle. Some of Italy's most important design houses are represented here, while a few have strayed to Via Manzoni and Via Montenapoleone (others – Flos, Alessi, Zanotta, Kartell – are also central). If testing the comfort of sofas has taken its toll, design-friendly respite is available at the historic Liberty-esque Taveggia Café on Via Visconti di Modrone (see Snack).

Armani Casa Angular, simple design – arguably minimalist, but Mr Armani prefers to call it 'essentialist'

B&B Italia A Wallpaper* favourite and the only one in Italy, with important pieces by important architects: Newson, Scarpa, Citterio and Piva

Bellora Traditional luxurious bed, table and bath linens

Cassina Sophisticated Italian furniture with designs from Gìo Ponti, Le Corbusier and Frank Lloyd Wright

Gervasoni Contemporary interiors boutique with Baxter, Flexform and own-brand pieces

Meritalia Contemporary furniture showroom and design studio with a 17-metre plasma screen and sci-fi 'Touch Me' automatic door

Via Manzoni, Centro

A historic street named after the 19th-century novelist Alessandro Manzoni, whose beautiful, perfectly preserved house is open to the public in nearby Via Morone. This street serves as the north edge of the *quadrilatero d'oro,* starting at the old arches of Porta Nuova at Piazza Cavour and with a whole block taken out by Armani-ville; other fashion boutiques are diluted among influential interiors shops, tourist shops and cafés since it's right in the tourist zone. Also on Via Manzoni is the important Museo Poldi Pezzoli; continue southwards for La Scala and the Duomo.

Armani Palace of Milan's fashion king, Giorgio Armani. A vast, clean, spare retail space with requisite giant catwalk screens on three floors, Armani has all your aesthetic needs covered – with fashion from his superluxe Giorgio Armani line, marginally cheaper Emporio Armani and Armani Jeans, artful flowers from Armani Fiori, logo-ed chocolates from Armani Dolci, fashionable coffee table books from Armani Libri, 'essentialist' (read minimalist) furniture and furnishings from Armani Casa and the latest must-have gadgetry from Armani Sony Gallery. Well-earned rests can be taken at the Emporio Armani Caffè and the Armani Nobu bar. Needless to say, Armani's kingdom continues into Via della Spiga, Via Sant' Andrea, Via Montenapoleone and Via Durini with stand-alone versions of some of these departments.

Artemide Dazzling contemporary lighting shop with colourful illumination in all imaginable forms
Barbara Bui Subdued, feminine fashion from Paris that's just a little bit dark

Da Driade Cutting-edge interiors quasi-gallery emporium with well-known Italian and international brands

Frette Italy's finest bed linen and loungewear company selling silk sheets, cashmere blankets and high thread counts

Mila Schön Understated fashion with simple lines, defined seams and reversible wool from Yugoslavian-born Milan-based fashion designer

Sawaya & Moroni Covetable contemporary chairs in bold colours and designs

Strenesse Quiet, sophisticated fashion from German designer Gabriele Strehle

Trussardi Classic leather goods, and seat of the Trussardi empire, including its sleek bar Marino alla Scala that's popular for *aperitivo*

Via Montenapoleone

'Montenapo' is another densely populated street, full of the most important Italian and international labels. Thankfully, ample reward is waiting at Café Cova, one of Milan's most celebrated patisseries that's chock-a with essential supplies to boost flagging sugar levels (see Snack). The historic Bagutta restaurant (see Eat) on Via Bagutta offers something more substantial, while chic brasserie Paper Moon on the same street delivers hot pizzas with fast, cold service.

Alberta Ferretti Romantic wispy silk chiffon dresses in pretty muted tones; her diffusion line Philosophy di Alberta Ferretti is just down the street

Cartier Three floors of French fine jewellery, watches and special pieces

Celine French glamour with bold, colourful designs

Christian Dior High voltage fashion on two floors by John Galliano

Dior Homme Hedi Slimane's cult skinny suiting in a ultra modern monochrome space, with a 'ghost' that follows you down the corridor-like changing room through heat-sensitive panels

Gucci Gucci's answer to everything from guitar plectrums to architect's sets plus fashion, luggage, accessories on four floors, all in a cool environment of grey stone, wenge wood and tinted mirrors

Hogan Tods' little brother: leather shoes and bags for all

La Murrina Modern Venetian glass from Murano

Loro Piana Cashmeres, leather accessories and shawls and scarves from classic Italian label

Miss Sixty Italy's young jeans brand bravely pitting itself against the big boys in a bold and bright boutique

Mont Blanc Watches, pens, fragrance and leather pieces, all with the famous snowy logo

Narciso Rodriguez Supersleek, superlatively tasteful New York high fashion to diet for

Pisa Orologeria Multi-brand watch specialists in a cream suede setting

Prada Separate men's and women's boutiques with Miuccia Prada's ever-coveted, modern yet retrospective designs

Ralph Lauren 1,500m^2 flagship on four floors in Italian neoclassical style, selling preppy American fashion

Valentino Classic Roman fashion for men and women with trademark red evening gowns.

Versace Bold, at times loud, glamorous fashion for men and women on five floors

Yves Saint Laurent Black lacquer angular space with two floors of exquisite elegance.

Via Sant' Andrea, Centro

The southern boundary of the *quadrilatero d'oro* is serried with high fashion, spilling over into Via Verri to the west. Rest Manolo-weary feet at the institutional Santa Lucia restaurant on Via S Pietro all'Orto (see Eat); get a caffeine fix at the Antica Cremeria San Carlo on Corso V Emanuele II (see Snack).

Alexander McQueen Stark white tunnel-like space with men's and women's fashion on two floors from the bad boy of British fashion

Banner Milan fashion bastion Biffi's more avant-garde brand selling hard-to-find Junya Watanabe, Proenza Schouler and Dries Van Noten

Burberry Checked classics and edgier designs from its Burberry Prorsum line on three floors

Costume National White Perspex space with understated monochrome men's and women's wear

Chanel The world of Chanel according to Karl Lagerfeld: fashion, accessories, perfumes and cosmetics; nearby is Haute Joaillerie in a bijou jewellery box of a shop

Ermenegildo Zegno Five floors of made-to-measure and off-the-peg Italian suiting, plus accessories, sports- and casual wear

Fendi The ground floor is devoted to Fendi's iconic handbags; glamorous men's and women's wear on the first floor

G. Lorenzi Famous gift shop for the man that has everything, selling exquisite pipes, cigar cutters, barber sets, walking canes, hipflasks etc.

Gianfranco Ferre Classic fashion and home to the Gianfranco Ferre Spa – the ultimate shopping pitstop

Hermes Luxury leather goods, silk scarves, watches, gifts and fashion designed by Jean Paul Gaultier

Jil Sander Gleaming minimalist space on two floors with equally minimal fashion for men and women

Marisa Multi-brand boutique selling Rochas, Issey Miyake, Comme des Garçons, Undercover and Balenciaga

Marni Future Systems-designed boutique containing edited highlights of Marni's nostalgic, naïf designs

Missoni High fashion in trademark stripey silk knits from the long-serving Milanese-based Missoni family

Moschino Playful feminine fashion in a playful setting with a chandelier made of glass slippers, *trompe l'oeil* furniture and enchanting window displays

Prada Sport 'Performance' fashion, ski- and surf wear and sporty accessories

OUTLETS

As a textiles capital, Milan is home to hundreds of factory outlet stores where designers sell off their dead stock and sample collections. The fashion-forward Milanese can spot last season's stock at a hundred paces and, generally, that's the distance they choose to keep from it, leaving rich pickings for foreigners. However, they're right to be snobbish about low-rent outlet shopping, usually a far cry from the luxurious boutiques of the *quadrilatero d'oro*. Many fashion designers have their own outlets, but listed here are the best multi-brand 'bargain basements'. All are a bag of known and unknown brands, stuffed to the rafters with a wide mix, from hidden treasures to clothes that have become part of the furniture. Reductions range from 30–70%; some stores even have January and July sales. Corso Buenos Aires is something of a discount zone, but the committed might like to travel to the out-of-town outlet villages. Professional bargain hunters should invest in 'Designer Bargains in Italy' (€16.50 from good bookshops; www.scoprioccasioni.it), which includes over 140 outlet listings in and around Milan.

10 Corso Como, Via Tazzoli, 3, Garibaldi

A less uptight and less expensive clearance house for Milan's uber-boutique; the most coveted pieces never make it this far.

D Magazine, Via Montenapoleone, 26, Centro, and Via Forcella, 13, Navigli

Milan's smartest factory outlet in slick, modern boutique format with avant-garde labels such as Helmut Lang, Martin Margiela, Ann Demeulemeester and Alexander McQueen, plus Alberta Ferretti, Prada, Gucci, YSL and the like. Stock is matched to the season, so in the summer it sells last summer's collections, and last winter's in winter. Efficient computerized systems mean that other sizes not visible on the shop floor can be tracked.

Il Salvagente, Via F Bronzetti, 16, Venezia

No-frills 600m^2 factory outlet with all the big names: Prada, Jimmy Choo, Valentino, Ralph Lauren, Dolce & Gabbana, Jil Sander

Matia, Piazza Mirabello, 4, Garibaldi

Classic styles, sportswear and cashmere from Prada, D&G, Paul Smith, Lora Piana, Armani, Roberto Cavalli and Ermenegildo Zegna

MARKETS

Head down to the markets to experience a rawer Milan. Pick up Italian antiques from Mercatone Dell'Antiquariato, a huge antiques market that lines the banks of the Navigli Grande canal with more than 350 stalls that seem to come from Milan's spring-cleaned attics, held on the last Sunday of every month. Curios include Venetian glass and chandeliers, old telephones and antique maps. La Fiera di Sinigaglia in Viale d'Annunzio is Milan's most important flea market, held every Saturday. Papiniano in Viale Papiniano is a popular open-air market on Saturdays, selling all sorts from junk to cut-price designer clothes.

play...

Milan's female-leaning fashion bias is somewhat redressed in this section by the city's more masculine passions for football and fast cars. Football is a religion in Milan, and shops are often decked out like shrines, every last corner covered with posters, calendars and flags. There's a citywide divide in loyalty between its famous rival teams AC (whose team colours are red and black) and Inter Milan (with a blue and black strip). There's no question of whom to support at Monza, home to the Italian Formula 1 Grand Prix: it's Forza Ferrari all the way for the *tifosi*, Italy's diehard fans. Back in Milan, you can hire your own Ferrari or race in a go-kart Grand Prix.

With its spotlight firmly fixed on fashion, furniture and entertainment, more sensible sporting activities seem to take place under the surface in Milan; sport and leisure seem all too humdrum by comparison. Nevertheless most Milanese are fine golfers and tennis players – usually behind the closed gates of exclusive private clubs. Milan has a small number of more egalitarian places for the proletariat minority.

More in keeping with glossy Milan is its select number of modern and luxurious spas. Bvlgari, Dolce & Gabbana and Gianfranco Ferré have all recently branched out into the well-being market. And recalling Milan's ancient roots are Aquae Calidae and Hammam Della Rosa – both spas inspired by Roman baths.

It is said that the only green in industrial Milan is its traffic lights. There are just three central parks for idling away an afternoon: Parco Sempione, the public gardens of Castello Sforzesco, Giardini Pubblici near Porta Venezia (both based on the classical English garden and full of trees, water features, historic buildings and picnicking families) and Parco Solari; with its glass-covered pool and poolside bar, it's a popular summer destination.

Thanks to its proximity to Italy's coastline resorts, lakes and mountains, most Milanese vacate the city whenever possible – in the summer to Portofino, Lake Como, Lake Garda and Lake Maggiore, while the winter is spent skiing in the Dolomites and Italian or Swiss Alps.

Lombardy's Lake District is beautiful and romantic, with a majestic Alpine backdrop dotted with historic villages and aristocratic dwellings. Lake Como, 35km north and the nearest, offers excellent water sports, horse-riding, mountain-biking and windsurfing (www.lakecomo.com). The top quarter of Lago di Garda – Italy's largest lake, 100km east of Milan, where mountain breezes roll in like clockwork – is reserved for wind sports; plenty of other pastimes (cycling, scuba-diving, tennis, water sports) are on offer all around the lake, as well as charming medieval towns and rugged scenery as it approaches the Dolomites (www.garda.com). Lake Maggiore, 50km west of Milan, borders the region of Piedmont and is equally picturesque and historic, with monasteries, fortresses, castles and islands, plus sailing, canoeing, waterskiing, hang-gliding and golf on offer (www.lagomaggiore.net). The Milanese also head to the medieval walled city of Bergamo (35km north-east of Milan) for its clean air and beautiful surrounding valleys (www.bergamo.it).

COOKERY

Q.B., Via C Farini, 70, Garibaldi
Tel: 02 690 065 46   www.quantobasta.net
Classes: 10am–1pm, 3–6pm, 7.30–10.30pm. Closed July and
August.

The Italians like to think they could teach foreigners a thing or
two about food. Who better than a two-Michelin-starred chef
and author of three Italian cookery books? Claudio Sadler of
Milan's Sadler restaurant (see Eat) runs Q.B., a gleamingly modern cookery school that offers one-off classes and longer courses. Q.B. stands for *quanto basta*, a culinary measure meaning
whatever is required, but since these lessons are in Italian only,
pupils might need a little more than this. Learn to cook in his
distinctive style that reworks traditional recipes into more delicate versions. There are two sorts of classes: *alta cucina* (haute
cuisine), usually led by Sadler himself where a generous flow of
tasters is delivered throughout the class; and *corso practico* which
is more basic and hands-on; at the end, students dine on their
own creations. For the confident, Sadler's Sunday Brunch slot
allows his disciples to invite (paying) guests to share in the fruits
of their labour. Advance booking essential.

CYCLING

Milan is a perfectly compact city for getting around by pedal
power. Unfortunately the city's tram tracks are perfectly
matched in size to bicycle wheels; avoid slipping into these –
once in, it's all over. Those charmingly cobbled streets can be
something of a bone-shaker on a bike, but it's worth it for the
exploring opportunities through the Navigli and surrounding
countryside. The best places to hire bikes from (and it will most
likely be the civilized 'sit up and beg' variety) are:

Rossignoli Cicli, Corso Garibaldi, 71
Tel: 02 804 960

AWS Bicimotor, Via Ponte Seveso, 33
Tel: 02 670 721 45

FAST CARS

It wouldn't do to buy up the stock of the *quadrilatero d'oro* and
then be seen returning to a tinny rental car. Much more fitting
would be to cruise Milan in a thoroughbred Italian motor
(although there's no promise of generous luggage space). Luxury
car hire company Vipernolo has a stable of Ferrari F355s, 360
Modenas and 430s and Lambourghini Murcièlagos and Gallardos,
as well as Porsches and 650–1,000cc Japanese motorbikes.

Vipernolo, Via Populonia, 6/8
Tel: 02 668 057 38 www.vipernolo.com

FOOTBALL

San Siro Football Stadium, Via Piccolomini, Monte Rosa
Tel: 02 404 2432 www.stadiosansiro.it

The hallowed turf of San Siro is a place of worship for both
Inter and AC Milan fans, whose teams have home rights on alter-
nate weeks. Of course the twice-yearly derby makes the most
fitting pilgrimage, but at any given game the atmosphere is
charged with deafening canons, hysterical crowds, footie songs
and swear words; the stadium is alight with flares and giant
sparklers. Be sure to join in when the crowd jumps up and down
– if you don't, it means you support the other team. AC and
Inter's illustrious history is commemorated in the on-site museum, which includes a tour of the dramatic stadium. Recently
restructured for the Italian World Cup in 1990, San Siro now has
a capacity of 85,000; at the end of a game, fans run down its
helter-skelter towers yelling 'Forza Milan!'/'Forza Inter!' Join
them in a post-match analysis in the crowded trams back to
Milan.

Inter tickets are sold at all branches of Banca Popolare di Milano or online at www.ticketone.it. AC Milan tickets are available at Milan Point Shop (Piazza XXIV Maggio; tel: 02 894 227 11), or all branches of Banca Cariplo. Touts sell outside the stadium.

GOLF

The Milanese are rather partial to a spot of golf, and the rolling countryside that surrounds Milan lends itself well to some fine golf courses that offer a good game and splendid views. Most courses and country clubs are strictly members-only, but a few will make exceptions, sometimes for Federation card-holders, and with handicap restrictions. Booking at the weekend is advisable.

Castello di Tolcinasco Golf & Country Club, Tolcinasco, Pieve Emanuele
Tel: 02 907 727 40 www.golftolcinasco.it
Open: 9am–5pm winter, 8.30am–6.30pm summer. Closed Mondays in winter.

Located 10km south of Milan, the Tolcinasco has four nine-hole courses against a backdrop of an imposing 16th-century castle. Three courses are at championship level, the other with easier starting tees for amateur players, all designed by Arnold Palmer. Modern amenities include a swimming pool, tennis courts, three putting greens and practice fields.

Golf Brianza Country Club, Cascina Cazzù, Usmate Velate
Tel: 03 968 9089 www.brianzagolf.it
Open: 8.30am–7.30 (5.30 in winter). Closed Tuesdays.

Situated 25km north-east of Milan in open countryside, the Brianza Country Club accepts non-members of all handicaps provided they have a good grasp of golfing etiquette. Karts, clubs and trolleys are available. Facilities include an 18-hole course, a driving range, putting green, pitching green and restaurant.

Golf Le Rovedine, Via Karl Marx, 18, Noverasco di Opera
Tel: 02 576 064 20   www.rovedine.com
Open: 8am–8pm (6pm in winter)

Lombardy's only public golf course, 7km from Milan, with a driving range and restaurant.

Molinetto Country Club, Strada Statale Padana Superiore, 11, Cernusco sul Naviglio
Tel: 02 921 051 28
Open: 9am–6pm. Closed Mondays.

Non-members with a maximum handicap of 36 are accepted to the Molinetto's 18-hole course on weekdays only. Facilities include a bar, restaurant and driving range.

HORSE-RACING

Ippodromo di Milano, Piazzale dello Sport angolo Via Piccolomini
Tel: 02 482 161 www.trenno.it

Right next to San Siro is Milan's horse-racing epicentre and home of the world's largest horse statue. There are two racetracks (or *hippodromi*): one for Roman Empire-style chariot races (from January to December and from June to mid-September), always at a trotting pace – hence the name 'Trotto'; and one for horse-racing ('Galoppo'; from March to November). The Milanese turn their noses up at the races – it's really a working-class preoccupation, comparable to going to the dogs; similarly it's a good place for a cheap flutter. Free entrance for women all year is an incentive to remove the large male bias (but that's yet to make any difference). At the entrance to the Galoppo is Da Vinci's vertiginous bronze horse, only built in 1999 when an American philanthropist took on the challenge to bring to life the seven metre high design that had physically defeated Da Vinci in the 15th century.

MOTOR RACING

Autodromo Nazionale Monza, Via Vedano, 5,
Parco di Monza, Monza
Tel: 03 924 821 www.monzanet.it
Open: 8am–7pm daily

Just 15km north-east of Milan is Monza, home to the Italian
Formula 1 Grand Prix and Ferrari's favourite battleground.
Monza has always been one of the fastest Formula 1 circuits
where speeds of up to 360km/h are reached despite new chi-
canes to slow it down. Set inside the historic walled Parco di
Monza, its original oval track was built in 1922 and has been
restructured into the high-speed circuit known today. This idyllic
forested park also contains a golf course, car museum, Olympic
swimming pool (open from June till the end of August) and a hip-
podrome. The old town of Monza itself and the Palazzo Reale
are also picturesque attractions. The Grand Prix is held on the
second Sunday in September and tickets – from €50 to more
than €500 – are available from ACI Milano (tel: 02 774 5400) or
direct from the racetrack. Track days and Ferrari club days can
also be arranged.

SCOOTER HIRE

When in Milan, do as the Milanese do – scoot around town. It's
best advised not to follow their approach to traffic laws, however (which are considered more as sensible suggestions than an
authority, particularly when it comes to wearing crash helmets,
red lights, and drinking and driving).

Biancoblu, Via Gallarate, 33
Tel: 02 308 2430 www.biancoblu.com

Happy Rent, Via Napo Torriani, 22
Tel: 02 667 101 76

SKIING

No self-respecting Milanese languishes in the city over winter weekends when in just one hour they could be posing on the slopes. Join the exodus for excellent Alpine skiing.

Livigno, 1,800–3,000m www.aptlivigno.it

Close to the border of Switzerland and 150km from Milan, this resort has 110km of runs and, because of its height, often has snow from November till May; with more green than black runs, there are fewer posers here. Climbing, ice-driving, horse-riding, dog-sledding and ice-skating are also available.

Madonna di Campiglio, 1,500m–2,580m www.campiglio.net

Located 220km from Milan in the Dolomites, this is where the scions of Milan's old money go. There are 90km of pistes, plus a natural ice rink, slalom stadium, tennis courts, bowling alley, dog sledding, paragliding, ice-climbing, snow-shoeing, holidays in igloos, mountain-biking on snow, and skiing till the end of April.

Sestriere, 2035m www.sestriere.it

Host to the Winter Olympics in 2006, this prestigious resort near Turin was purpose-built in the 1930s; its massive snow-making facilities mean it opens in early December with access to over 400km of pistes, plus tennis, dog-sledding, an outdoor skating rink, night-skiing and parapenting.

SPAS

Aquae Calidae, Via Santa Sofia, 14, Navigli
Tel: 02 584 302 69 www.aquaecalidae.it
Open: 11am–10pm (8pm Sat, Sun). Closed Wednesdays and throughout August.

Classicists will appreciate Aquae Calidae (Latin for 'hot water') – a contemporary interpretation of the ancient Roman baths, which takes you through the ancient and now fashionable ritual of hot–cold therapy. Roman-like indulgence is also encouraged (the motto is '*Salus et Otium*' – 'health and idleness') but of course it's minus the bacchanalia and plus super-modern architecture. Get into character with a muslin toga in the *apodyterium* (changing room), then slip into the *balneae pensiles* (shower rooms) to wash under rain showers. The *tepidarium* is a Roman forum-like hall in travertine marble heated to 36°C, with tiered steps around a central fountain. It's not quite milk baths and peeled grapes, but artful bowls of dried fruit and the restorative sound of running water capture the mood. Next is a 15-minute massage and Adriatic sea-salt scrub by a *tractator* (masseur), followed by the 50°C *calidarium*, a steam room that's scented with eucalyptus in the winter, fruits in the summer. The *frigidarium* is not so much a plunge pool but an icemaker than churns out crushed ice that you voluntarily rub over yourself – quite literally a refresher in classical civilization.

Bulgari Spa, Via Privata Fratelli Gabba, 7b, Garibaldi
Tel: 02 805 805 200 www.bulgarihotels.com
Open: 7.30am–9pm daily

The exclusive Bulgari Hotel's spa is a fittingly five-star affair. Some 300,000 real gold mosaic tiles line its indoor pool while sun-loungers the size of double beds look out onto its private gardens. Turkish baths contained within a large emerald glass cube, plus refreshments supplied by Bulgari's hotel chef, add to the luxurious ambience of a modern-day Roman palace. Holistic treatments are selected from around the world (including Balinese massages, Indian head massages, Swedish massages and so on) and are administered with E'SPA products and Ayurvedic aromatherapy. Twenty-first-century ailments are relieved with treatments like the Jet Lag Eliminator and After-Shopping Treatment, all in a serene candlelit setting with conversation conducted *sotto voce*. Day access to the pool and steam room is available from €55 and guests can have treatments in their rooms. Bulgari's bar also offers excellent *aperitivo* – perfect for undoing all your good work in the spa.

Set within the Sicilian-style courtyard of the Dolce & Gabbana menswear flagship store is a traditional barbershop and frill-free, male-friendly spa where Stefano and Domenico themselves are regulars. The small spa (called 'Grooming', not, say, 'Beauty') is functional to the point of being clinical, all clean and modern with white Carrera marble, frosted glass and white lacquer. It offers high-tech beauty treatments for men and women such as skin peeling, massages, facials, depilation and mani-/pedicures. The barbershop – with lacquered walnut panelling, green marble flooring and two repro barber's chairs – harks back to the classic cut-throat shave that starts and finishes with hot towels and, of course, Dolce & Gabbana cologne. You could always ask for a Domenico haircut, which would leave you with a grade 1, but if in doubt, think it over in the Dolce & Gabbana Martini Bar – it's also a bit of a showcase for the barber who attends to the staff's grooming.

Something of an inner sanctum in the heart of the bustling *quadrilatero d'oro*, Gianfranco Ferré's small and exclusive spa is a 'journey into relaxation' (via his fashion boutique). Dark with black marble and Bisazza mosaics and with an ambient temperature of 33°C, it's immediately soporific. The wind-down starts with a snooze on an indoor sun-lounger that looks out onto the small private garden, followed by a float in the Vitality pool – a small black swimming pool heated to 36°C, with a jacuzzi and swan neck fountains (like huge high-pressure taps) for hydromassage; chromotherapeutic lighting adds a little *je ne sais quoi*. Then take a scented rain or mist shower before entering the black and gold mosaic mud chamber where marine mud is

applied. Holistic massages, facials and mani/pedicures are available
in two pristine treatment rooms in walnut and cream leather (all
products by E'SPA). There are separate men's, women's and
mixed timetables and reservation is recommended; four-hour
packages including lunch are available, powernaps are
unavoidable.

Habits Culti, Via A Mauri, 5, Sempione
Tel: 02 485 175 88 www.habitsculti.it
Open: 10am–10pm daily

This chic lifestyle concept store, with its own furniture range,
chocolate and flower departments and design consultancy,
recently added a spa to its repertoire. In a trademark soft
palette of cream marble and teak decking gently lit with candles
and soft spotlights, the basement spa is pleasingly tranquil; even
magazines are removed so as to encourage complete relaxation
(reading would be too much like work). There are two twin spas
for men and women, so no coupling here (though the lovesick
can meet in the hammam). All treatments are holistic and influ-
enced by Ayurveda and the Orient, and are modified to suit city
lifestyles (for example, speed massages and oil-free head massages) and city vices (try their three-day 'Purify' treatment for
detoxing, quitting smoking or weight loss). The Spa Café has just
opened, but if retox is desired, there's a direct walk-through to
the equally chic bar/restaurant Noy that's entirely furnished with
Culti pieces.

Hammam Della Rosa, Viale Abruzzi, 15, Venezia
Tel: 02 294 116 53 www.hammamdellarosa.com
Open: midday–10pm Tues–Fri; 11am–7pm Sat, Sun (last entry 2½
hours before closing). Closed Mondays and throughout August.

The elegant and modern Hammam Della Rosa is a (rather circular) Italian take on the Arabic interpretation of ancient Roman
baths. This process includes a *tepidarium* (a 32°C relaxation
chamber), a *calidarium* (a 45°C steam room scented with essential oils) and a *frigidarium* (at 28°C, just cooler than ambient tem

perature), with various massages and scrubs till your skin squeaks along the way. There are separate hammams for men and women, authentic in every last detail with Tunisian marble, Persian music, and Moroccan and Algerian staff administering Lebanese mud wraps, Syrian olive oil washes and almond and rose oil massages from the hammam's own line of organic products. The ritual continues into the Café Letterario (literary café) where Moroccan mint tea and *baklava* is served on silk tasselled cushions at low tables, decorated with scattered rose petals and floating candles. Right-on conversation with the politically aware management – usually on Third World poverty and women's rights – will leave you cleansed and smelling of roses.

WATER SPORTS

Idropark Fila, Via Circonvallazione Est, Segrate
Tel: 02 702 009 02   www.provincia.milano.it/idroparkfila
Open: 9am–9pm daily

This artificial lake near Linate airport was originally built in 1930 as a hydroplane airport; it's now effectively Milan's mini Riviera. Set in over 1.6m square metres, this leisure park is half in the woods and half on the lake, measuring 2.5km long and 5km wide and filled with clean, cold Lombardy spring water lined with sandy beaches. From the beginning of April till the end of October, Idropark Fila (or Idroscalo as it is still known, pre-Fila sponsorship) is Milan's summer playground, with water sports (canoeing, rowing, waterskiing, swimming and sailing – on rare breezy days), mountain-biking, blading, tennis, climbing and cross-country running. By night, it's packed out with cool kids (and mosquitoes) as Milan's nightlife migrates from the city centre to Idroscalo's bars, restaurants, clubs and big-name concerts. Clubs of note are Café Solaire, Dieci 57 and Punta dell'Est. Thanks to Linate's air traffic, there are plenty of Bill-and-Ted style plane-spotting opportunities. Ice-skating is available in the winter.

info...

DRIVING

Driving in Milan can be frustrating because of complicated decongestion measures, impossible parking and the Italians' wilful disobedience of traffic laws. Sundays are often designated car-free days and many parts of the city are only accessible to residents on any given day. Street-cleaning days where cars are forbidden from parking on one side of the street don't help to ease parking problems in Milan: the best option is find a car park. The Milanese usually indulge in creative parking – up the kerb, double-parked, at a junction; it is said that bumpers were designed for Italian drivers. Most drive fast (and are impatient with those who don't), tailgate, and drink and drive.

MONEY

Milan supposedly has more banks than churches, so accessing cash in euros is very easy. What is less straightforward is the *cassa* system, which is the norm in most bars, cafés and clubs – where goods must be paid for at the till first. Don't join an hour-long bar queue to be sent to the back to buy tokens.

NAVIGATION

Milan is a perfect-sized city for a visitor – most sights can easily be reached by foot and 5km is considered a great way to go to for a plate of pasta. The Duomo is right at the heart of Milan and circling it are concentric ring roads, variously punctuated with historic city gates (Porta Romana, Porta Venezia, for example). Street numbers on the main roads increase going away from town. *Angolo* means corner and *bis* means next door.

PUBLIC HOLIDAYS

While the Milanese are renowned for their strong work ethic, like all Italians they know how to reward themselves. The whole of August is a holiday for most of Milan, as is Christmas to Epiphany (6 January). There are public holidays on New Year's Day, Epiphany, Easter Monday, Liberation Day (25 April), May Day, Republic Day (2 June), Feast of the Assumption (15 August), All Saints Day (1 November), Feast of Sant' Ambrogio (7 December), Christmas Day and Boxing Day.

PUBLIC TRANSPORT

Milan has an excellent, and inexpensive, public transport system: the metro is straightforward with three lines and an easily navigable map; trains run from 6am to midnight every 5 minutes. Tickets are valid for one trip on the metro or 75 minutes on buses and trams, and must be purchased before boarding and be stamped at ticket gates or on board. Standard tickets cost €1 and can be purchased from newsagents, tobacconists and machines at larger stops. All-inclusive subway, bus and tram tickets cost €3 for 24 hours, available at Duomo and Stazione Centrale metro stations.

SMOKING

Since January 2005, it is illegal to smoke in public indoor spaces in Milan.

TAXIS

Because of Milan's pollution problem, taxis don't cruise around the city, but park up at ranks, designated by a white sign that reads TAXI in black. All licensed taxis are white in colour and run on a meter; there's a surcharge out-side normal hours (6am–9pm) and a higher tariff for three passengers or more. Taxi drivers are mostly extremely honest and will often round down a fare and not expect much of a tip. An average price to Linate airport is €15. Taxis can be booked by phone: the best are Radio Taxi (tel: 02 8585) and Code Blue (tel: 02 4040).

TELEPHONES

The international dialling code for Italy is +39. The local code for Milan is 02; if dialling from outside the country, the code for Milan is +39 02.

TIPPING

The Milanese don't tip much in restaurants (waiters are apparently not on the minimum wage here, and certainly most don't seem to be encouraged by the incentive of potential tippers). It's usual to leave a token quantity of coins (up to €5), although foreigners are still expected to be more generous (up to 10%). All restaurants charge a cover (or *coperto*) of up to €5.

Hg2 Milan

index

index